NINE DAYS IN ITALY

NINE DAYS IN ITALY

The Highs and Lows of Driving Through Italia on Your Own

by

Warren Landrum

&

Carol Landrum

Warland Books

Grand Prairie, Texas

NINE DAYS IN ITALY
Published by:
Warland Books
2791 Explorador
Grand Prairie, TX 75054
Warrenglandrum@hotmail.com

Warren Landrum, Publisher / Editorial Director
Yvonne Rose/Quality Press, Production Coordinator

ALL RIGHTS RESERVED

Paperback ISBN #: 978-0-9787355-3-1
Ebook ISBN #: 978-0-9787355-4-8
Library of Congress Control Number: 2016960529

Dedication

This book is dedicated to our granddaughter Mia, who has re-energized us and given us a totally new focus on life. It's Mia's World!

Mia, we want you to always live life to the fullest and enjoy it, and yourself, as much as Nana and Papa Warren do.

Nana and Papa Warren love you Mia ☺ !!!

Table of Contents

Introduction

Have you ever wondered what it would be like to drive through a foreign country half-way around the world on a nice, relaxing vacation, where they speak no English? Or are you the type that prefers the kind of vacation where everything is pretty much laid out for you and provided for – like on a cruise or an all-inclusive land-based vacation? Well, my wife and I had been pretty much of the latter persuasion over the last couple decades, taking many cruises throughout the Caribbean, mixing in an all-inclusive to Mexico or Jamaica, or maybe the Bahamas every now and then. But this year, I convinced her that we needed to go on an adventure, and just go on a trip where we could go at our own pace. And, wouldn't you know it? Shortly after that little chat, I got an e-mail alert from one of the travel sites I subscribe to – Great Value Vacations. They were advertising 10 days in Italy for a ridiculously low price. For just a little more than what it would normally cost for just the airfare to fly to Europe, they were offering accommodations outside of Rome, in Tuscany, and outside of Venice, in addition to throwing in a car! I think what sealed the deal for us was Tuscany. My wife had always been in love with Tuscany. We have watched that movie, "Under the Tuscan Sun" together, and she even has a few paintings on our walls that depict some of the Tuscan countryside. So, it was on!!!

So… what we will attempt to do in this book is to tell you the story of our trip. Hopefully, if I do my job, it will be told in such a way that you will be crying with us as we are going through our first Near-Death experience up in the

1

mountains in Tuscany, and you will feel some of the same jaw-dropping, OMG emotions that we had when we got our first glimpse of *The Sistine Chapel* in Rome or Michelangelo's *David* in the Galleria dell' Accademia in Florence or *The Leaning Tower* in Pisa.

We also hope that you pick up on some of the little details and nuances that we did not know about, so with this knowledge, you will be able to overcome some of the little hiccups and road-bumps that we encountered along our journey. And while this is not necessarily a travel-guide, but more of an adventure story, we still will be giving some travel tips up front because we feel that seeing how we prepared for our trip was all a part of the total adventure, in addition to the actual recounting of our various trials, tribulations, and triumphs.

So, are you ready? Buckle up, hang on, and let's DO this thing!!

Ciao Baby!!!

Trip Preparation

Before going on ANY vacation, I like to be as prepared as I can in regards to having an idea of what the vacation sites and locales have to offer. In some cases, I already have a general idea, maybe just from what I remember from history classes, or from seeing vacation brochures or travel shows on television, or from having talked to people who have been there. But since time is a precious resource when you are on vacation, I like to make sure that we maximize our time by doing the research and due-diligence ahead of time. More times than not, during these fact-gathering sessions, I find out many more interesting things about the places that I did not already know – both good things, and in some cases, travel tips that warn you about things to look out for - and that allows me to further plan the trip in a way so that we can maximize our time and enjoyment. Of course, things come up, and the spontaneity of the moment and surprises always come into play, but most times, these things just make the trip more memorable.

So… with that said, I'd like to share with you some of the things we did beforehand to try and be as prepared as possible for the 10-day trip to Italy which we were on from September 12th through September 21st.

Once I got "buy-in" from my wife Carol that she was good with this trip, I immediately got on line and booked it with Great Value Vacations, locking it in before those great rates got away from us! Then I started to do my research. We had a copy of *The Complete Idiot's Travel Guide: Planning Your Trip to Europe* in our library, so I pulled it out and started going through the chapters that talked about Rome, Tuscany, and Venice. With each page that I read, my excitement and anticipation grew more and more. But at one point, when they started talking about some of the costs and prices for various things like bus tickets, and about the currency in general, I noticed they were talking about liras as the unit of currency. I knew that Italy was now using the Euro as their currency, as were other members of the European Union. So, I looked at the publication date of the book, and saw that it was 1998, which pre-dated the actual date that the first Euro currency was used by about a year. So, with that tidbit of knowledge, I thought that perhaps it might be wise to get some reference material that was a little more current, since we are now in 2016. So off to Barnes and Nobles I went, and before you could say 'Michelangelo,' I had a copy of *"Fodor's Travel: Italy 2016"* in my hands. Now we were in business!!!

I would HIGHLY recommend *Fodor's* as both a pre-travel resource for your trip, and also as a handy guide to review nightly once you get to your destination. Once you are actually there and get a "lay of the land," some of the items contained in this guidebook may be more meaningful, especially if you will be in a city or area for more than one day, and have already been out and about before reviewing it in the evening. Some of the main sections I like to dig into for each city or area are *Top Attractions, Top Experiences, Getting Around, and Eating and Drinking Well*. And once you have honed in on some of the things you want to see, like maybe The Vatican in Rome, there are detailed sections about that specific item that will allow you to get a hint of some of the things to look for when at that attraction. It's all about doing all you can to make the experience as memorable as possible once you get there. Throughout each section, Fodor's has placed their *Fodor's Choice* stamp in front of items that they have found to be particularly significant or enjoyable. These include tourist attractions, shopping areas, and foods or restaurants that they highly recommend.

As I talked to people and let them know we were going to Italy on vacation, a recurring theme came up. Just about everyone I spoke with said something like, "Yeah, when you're in Rome, you better watch out for pick-pockets." Hmmm... All these people saying the same thing must mean something! So, I told Carol about this (probably should NOT have, as it made her a little apprehensive about the trip) in the interest of full disclosure. But so many people brought this up, that I thought I needed to do something about it to prepare. So, I started thinking about maybe I should wear a shoulder-holster type wallet under my shirt, or something like that, if it existed. Better safe than sorry, right? So off I went to my computer and good old Google. Sure enough, when I entered Shoulder Holster Wallet a bunch of them came back. I saw a couple of them on Amazon.com that had some pretty good reviews and were relatively inexpensive ($50 or less), so about a week before we were to leave, I wound up ordering two of them – one for Carol, and one for me. Forewarned is forearmed, and once they arrived a couple days before our departure flight, I felt much better. Again, it's all about the preparation!

Let the Journey Begin

This trip started out on a positive note for me for one simple reason – the departure time of our flight from DFW Airport to O'Hare Field in Chicago. Our plane was scheduled to leave at 2:20pm, which meant that we did not have to be at the airport until around 12:30 or so, which means we did not have to get up early for a pre-dawn flight. It seems that most of our flights for vacations over the years have always been early-morning for some reason. So, I really enjoyed the fact that we could have a leisurely morning and just take our time. And the fact that our daughter was driving us to the airport was bonus. So, after the 25-minute drive from home to the airport, all we had to do was hop out of the car at the Departure terminal, unload our bags and walk a few steps inside the terminal to the Ticket Kiosk. Then we were ready for Freddy.

After checking our bags and walking over to the Security line, we got another pleasant surprise. The agent waved us both over to the line at the left, telling us we were Pre-Select. I did not really know what this meant, other than it was just a short line. So, I took my shoes and belt off, and walked toward the metal detector/scanner. I was somewhat surprised when they told me I could have left them on, and when I looked back, I saw that Carol was approaching me with her shoes still on. I didn't learn until we returned from the trip that preselection was part of a three-tiered TSA program that went into effect in 2013, in which randomly selected passengers got chosen for "expedited, standard or enhanced screening" in which they would not have to remove shoes or belts, or laptops from their bags. All I knew was that we got through that short line being treated as though we were "special." I took this as an omen of good things that were to come on our trip. But the effects of the omen sure didn't last long, as you will see shortly!

We arrived at O'Hare on schedule, after about a 2.5-hour flight. The flight was without incident or turbulence. As we were touching down, my wife asked me if it felt good to be home. I was born and raised in East Chicago, Indiana, about 25 miles from downtown Chicago. But I surprised myself when the words that came out of my mouth were, "Not really." I guess the fact that my parents and brother were all dead, and my sister was living in Atlanta, made it seem as though this wasn't really home any more. That was the first time I ever really had that feeling. Strange…

Anyhow, we deplaned and found a Departure Screen so we could find out what terminal and gate our connecting flight was going to be at, since they did not announce it on the plane. I had checked before we left Dallas and it said we were arriving at B18 and our next flight was leaving from B17. But they changed on us and we had to depart from E4, which meant we had to take the long walk toward the middle of the Terminal Complex and then hook a left. I was kind of glad we did that, as it turned out, because I was able to recapture some of my childhood memories of going on field trips to the Field Museum of Natural History, when we turned the corner and a big dinosaur skeleton on loan from the museum came into view. My wife got excited and said, "Wait, wait. I have to take a picture for Mia, so she can see this." Mia is our 2-year old granddaughter. As my eyes fell off the dinosaur, they landed on one of the concession stands to the right of him. It was a Garrett Popcorn stand! Garrett's is a gourmet popcorn originating in Chicago, and I had not had any since the last time we were in Chicago a few years ago. So, I went over and got a large bag of the Garrett Mix (mixture of Caramel Corn and Cheese Popcorn) and we headed to our gate.

When we got to the gate, Carol said she had her first realization that we were heading to a foreign country where people did not speak English, when she started talking to a fellow traveler who looked like he could have been Italian, and he just kind of nodded and ignored her. Shortly after, the guy's wife came up, and Carol started talking to her. She had an accent, which turned out to be Cuban. When Carol said that she had been chatting with her husband, the woman asked, "Did he answer?" She said that would have been strange since he spoke no English! We all had a good laugh at that, and shortly after they called our group for boarding.

On the Plane to Rome

As we walked toward our seats in Row 44 (two rows from the back), the excitement started bubbling up in me again. Not only were we finally about to take off for our 9.5-hour flight from O'Hare to Rome's Leonardo da Vinci Airport in Fiumicino, but we also would not have that far to walk to get to the restrooms, which was not an insignificant detail on a long Trans-Atlantic flight such as this!

The aircraft was a big Boeing 777, the one with three seats across on both sides and 3-across in the middle as well. We had one of the non-middle rows, me in the aisle, and Carol in the middle. Our seatmate was already there when we got to our row. She had a pleasant smile and a friendly face. We said our greetings and settled in.

After we got airborne and leveled off at around 35,000 feet, Carol and the lady, Rachel, started chatting. It turned out that Rachel was a professor out of Atlanta and a frequent traveler to Italy, and knew the country quite well, having lived up in Tuscany for a year, at one point. She was a Painting Instructor and was actually going on this trip to have a Painting Retreat up in Tuscany, with a group of 12 students, some of whom were traveling with her. As the conversation with her continued, at one point, she kind of leaned in toward Carol, and said under her breath, "You guys need to be very careful in Rome in regard to pickpockets." There it was again – that recurring theme.

She went on to say that a lot of times, the pickpockets worked in gangs, and most of them were what she called "gypsy" kids. She said that they would do the bump-and-distract maneuvers, where one kid would bump into you, and another one or two would then hit just about every pocket you had on you in the blink of an eye. She also told us she had actually seen instances where a group of kids would run up to an unsuspecting tourist and surround the person with cardboard, and then do their dastardly deed. Wow!

As Rachel leaned back, I saw that she actually had a leather pouch/belt already strapped around her waist underneath her blouse. She explained that her pouch was a special one that blocked sophisticated thieves who used long-range scanners to try and do identity theft of people's credit card and passport numbers. So, just in case we had forgotten to be wary of pickpockets before we got to Rome, it was definitely back on our consciousness again.

At the Airport in Rome

W e had left Dallas at around 2:20pm on Monday, and when we arrived in Rome, it was about 10:30am Tuesday morning. That was because of about a total of 12 hours flying time and the fact that Rome is seven hours ahead of Dallas.

After we got our bags and cleared Customs in Rome, the next piece of business was to find the Hertz Car Rental office, so we could pick up our car. I must say the Rome airport was quite hectic and chaotic, to say the least. There were people going every which way, and to top it off, there was construction going on. As we looked around for some signs to lead us in the right way, we saw our seat-mate Rachel, and her niece Ann and sister Becky, who had traveled over with her to assist with her Painting retreat. Ann must have been in her late 20's or early 30's and she looked very excited. We exchanged pleasantries with her, and she told us something that would prove to be prophetic during this trip, to some degree. You'll see what I mean later. She said, "I learned a long time ago to have low expectations, then I won't be disappointed. Then if anything good happens, I'll be pleasantly surprised."

At the time, I thought she was just being pessimistic, but again – her words would hit home with us later.

So, we finally spotted a sign that said "Car Rentals" and wound up catching an elevator up to the 2nd floor to get to the Hertz office. I took a number and waited our turn, and before long, we were at the desk. The young lady that assisted us spoke pretty good English, so that was a relief. I told her where we were going, and she gave me a map and kind of explained how to get there from here, even circling key turnoff points and exits. It looked pretty straightforward, and I felt pretty confident, especially since I had also gotten on MapQuest before we left home, and printed out a route map and directions. So, all that was left was to go pick up our vehicle and hit the road.

We headed downstairs and across the street to where the rental cars were. We found the Hertz office and I went inside and gave the lady my paperwork. She gave me the keys and just for grins, I also asked her for directions to get to our hotel. She gave pretty much the same route as the lady upstairs had; so again, I felt pretty good. I asked her if the car had a GPS, and she said "No." My mistake was not following this response up by asking if she had any cars that DID have GPS. We walked over to the car, which was just a couple aisles over, and saw that they had given us a big blue Volvo SUV. I had upgraded to an automatic before leaving the States. I was glad that we would not be getting one of those little Fiats or something like that with little to no leg room or cargo space for our suitcases. We were pretty much riding in luxury.

We put our bags in the back and got in and I put the key in the ignition and pushed the button to start the engine. I noticed that there was a little strip of paper that said DIESEL, attached to the dashboard. I drove over to the rental exit station where we would do the final walk-through, marking where the car was damaged. I noticed two things when I put the car in Park to talk to the attendant. One, the car seemed to cut off, and two, this attendant did not speak any English. I tried to tell him that I thought something was wrong with the car, since it cut off, but he just gave me that "No Engleesh" spiel, and started walking around the car. A little exasperated at this point, I showed him the additional two scuff marks that Carol and I had found, and just got back in the car, and cranked it up, and headed out into Italy!

The Road to Hotel Villa Vecchia
- Lost in Rome

As soon as we left the airport car rental garage, I knew we were in trouble. I had given both the directions I printed form home, and the map that the Hertz agents had given me, to Carol. But I neglected to go over them with her before we pulled out, which was a big mistake. So, here we were trying to read all these signs, which were mostly in Italian obviously, looking for names of places and roads and exits that we saw on our maps. Talk about instant stress! The main things we knew were that we were supposed to get on the A1 Autostrade South Napoli via something called the Grande Raccordo Anulare (G.R.A.). Well, as we were driving along, I thought I saw an exit off to my right that said something about the G.R.A., but the road straight ahead said something about the A1, so I rolled the dice and kept going straight. Wrong Move! A few miles further down the road, and we actually entered what appeared to be the city limits of Rome and crossed into the city. The highway became a city street at that time, and we were officially lost for the first time. There was a lot of screaming going on inside the car at the time, and that did not help anything. So, I knew that somehow, I had to turn around and head back toward the airport and start over. We decided to try to get back to the Car Rental place and see if we could get a car with a GPS. So, that was our goal.

I somehow found a place up ahead where I was able to make a left turn on the city streets, and started heading back in the general direction of where I thought the airport was. We got lucky. Within a couple minutes, I saw a sign talking about the A1 that pointed to the right, so I veered off on that road, and a couple minutes later started seeing landmarks, like a Sheraton hotel, that I had seen coming down. We were on track! In about 15 minutes, we were back on the airport grounds. But now finding our way back to the Hertz Car Rental return place was our mission. We had been in Italy all of maybe two hours, at that point. I kept going and followed a sign to what I thought was the car rental place, but wound up on a side road behind what looked like some kind of convention center. I circled around behind that sucker and got back on the road and went around a roundabout, and there it was – Car Rental Returns. After going a little past the entrance, I made a U-turn and went up the ramp to the 2nd floor, and there we were – right back where we had started from about 45 minutes or so ago!

I parked the car. Carol stayed in it. I went over to the office. The lady that had given me the car was busy with another customer; so, another agent assisted me. When I told her that we needed a car with a GPS, she looked at my key, and said that one should have one. She walked me outside and got a couple of her guys to go over to the car with me. The first guy showed us the button on the dashboard/display monitor that said GPS, but he could not figure out how to operate it. But the 2nd guy was able to show us how to get it up and going, and more importantly, how to look at our destination address, and determine which part of it was the City, which was the Street, and which was the Street Number. These first two items were not easy to figure out, because as we were finding out, the addresses of all the lodgings we were going to, had a City component, and a municipality and region; and the streets listed were sometimes not really the street you needed to put in. Trying to decipher these addresses would be the cause of much grief over the next few days, especially leaving our hotel in the Rome area and heading up to Tuscany.

So anyway, I looked at the address of the Hotel Villa Vecchia, where we were going, and punched it in. The only thing was that it did not take the street number of 49, which we wanted to enter, so I just punched in 48. At that point, I figured if it could get me that close, I would be happy. Thirty minutes later, we pulled up to our home for the next couple days – the Hotel Villa Vecchia, Via Frascati 49, Monte Porzio Catone, Italy – right around the corner from and right past Via Frascati 48. Whew!!!

We pulled onto the grounds and at first sight, it was a nice, quaint property. I guess the reason it appeared so quaint is that it was built in 1560 under the direction of Cardinal Giovanni Ricci of Montepulciano. The Villa has quite an auspicious history, as Pope Gregory XIII (Pope from 1572 – 1585) sometimes used it as his summer residence.

We had to drive through a large entry-way, and go up a slight incline to get to the main entrance/baggage drop-off point. The building was a light mustard-yellow color, and we could see the green shutters that bordered all the bedroom windows. Across the highway, looking out from the hotel, there was a beautiful view of the mountains and another town across the valley on the other side.

But as we went inside and approached the front desk, this was the first example of where not having high expectations came into play. From both my wife's and my joint travels around the United States and the world, and my business travels, we are used to having first-rate service in all areas when traveling. That obviously includes the initial greeting/First Impression. Now bear in mind that we had just gone through quite a stressful little mini-adventure just to get to the hotel, so I figured on at least receiving a warm smile, and a 'Buon Giorno.' Wrong. The young lady who greeted me was not very warm, and quickly just looked up my reservation, pulled the room key, and pointed me in the general direction to our room. Welcome to Italy!! So, anyhow, after going down a wrong hall, which was also in the direction in which she had pointed, we doubled back, and saw another hallway and some signs pointing the way to the various rooms, so we were finally able to get to our room. The room number itself, was easy enough to remember – 1011, which was my birthday – October 11th, for what that's worth…

First Dinner in Italy

After we got settled in our room, and freshened up after a long, long day, it was about time for dinner. We followed the 'Ristorante' sign toward the back of the property and wound up in a narrow hallway with a low-watt lighting. It led to a spiral staircase that led to the lower level, and on our way down, we passed an elderly couple on their way up. As we got closer to the bottom, we could hear the sounds of laughter and silverware against plates. When we reached the bottom, we looked to our left and at the far side of a medium-sized dining area was a table full of mostly old men and women, having a great time. There must have been about a dozen or so people at that table. We waited for a maître d' or someone to seat us, but none did. At one point, a man came out of what appeared to be the kitchen area carrying a tray, but he just walked right on past us without even acknowledging us. After a couple more minutes, I decided to go back upstairs to the main desk and see if we could get them to get someone to wait on us. The same young woman who had checked us in was at the desk, and when I told her what the problem was, she got on the phone and called someone and then told me "No Problem. Go back downstairs and someone will be there."

Sure enough, when I got back downstairs, there was a gentleman talking to Carol, and he took us around the way to the other side of the room where they had more intimate tables-for-two, and he seated us. There was one other couple on that side, but they finished their meal and left shortly after we got there.

I ordered some type of beef strips over spinach dish, which was tasty enough, and Carol ordered the Roast Suckling Pig. She said it was a little too crunchy and salty for her liking, so our first meal in Italy got less than rave reviews. The local wine that was recommended by the waiter – a Frascati Red, was very good. So, after a long day, and two full bellies, we retired to our room to get ready for our big trip into Rome on the next day. On the way to the room, we passed through a nice lounge area that they had upstairs and got our first taste of what we would be seeing tomorrow, as there were two marble busts adorning a table toward the back of the room. We briefly stopped at the front desk to make arrangements to be taken to the train station in Frascati early the next day, and we were off to the Land of Nod!

9/14 – Rome

As we got into the shuttle that the hotel provided to take us to the Train Station in Frascati, I finally felt like a tourist. We were actually on our way into Rome to see some of the magnificent artifacts, buildings, and works of art that we had read about for years or seen only on television or in the movies. I mean, this was the land of Charlton Heston and Ben Hur, for goodness sakes!

Having reviewed a little bit about Rome in *Fodor's* before drifting off to sleep the prior evening, and reading about all that there was to see and do in Rome, I knew that the famous saying about Rome, "Roma, non basta una vita" (Rome, a lifetime is not enough), certainly was true. But we were determined to hit as many of the highlights as we could.

As we undertook the 10-15-minute ride to Frascati and the train station, we started to get an idea of how crazy the locals drove. As we approached one roundabout, in what looked like the center of town, there was just a mad rush and it seemed like everyone tried to enter it at the same time from all directions. The only time I had ever seen anything like that was over in Paris on the Champs-Elysees.

When we arrived at the train station, we had to get our tickets from a ticket machine. Trenitalia, the state-owned train system, wound up being the one we would use in all our stops, to get from our local outposts into the main cities of Rome, Florence, Pisa, and Venice.

We got another clue about how prevalent pickpocketing was in Rome as soon as I entered my credit card in the ticket machine. After you chose your language, the first thing the machine told you, in a loud, clear voice was to "beware of pickpockets." I was sure glad I had my wallet-holster on!

The tickets were surprisingly cheap at a little over 2 Euros per person, for a one-way ticket for the 30-minute ride from Frascati to Roma Termini, which is the main train station in Rome. Frascati is about 20 kilometers (12 miles) southeast of Rome. The exchange rate for Euros to US Dollars during our trip was 1 Euro = roughly $1.10 USD. So, the tickets were roughly $2.50 USD one-way.

Once we boarded the train, we saw that it was multi-level. You could either go down a couple steps to get to a lower level, or up about three or four steps to get to an upper level. We headed for the upper deck in our car, but it was full so we wound up coming back down to the main level. This was also the regular commuter train, and since we were heading in at around 8:30 am on a Wednesday morning, there were quite a few businessmen on the train. There were about five stops between Frascati and Roma Termini.

What I loved about these trains is that they were on rubber tires instead of metal, so when they pulled into the stations, it was like a Whisper jet, unlike the clackety-clack you get when riding American trains (at least the last time I rode American trains, it sounded like that. But that was decades ago). They were also pretty prompt for the most part, usually arriving and departing within a minute or so of the scheduled times. My wife said they were so clean and spacious, and un-crowded, that she thoroughly enjoyed them. She had not been a train person, with this only being

21

about her 3rd time, and thoroughly enjoyed it. She was also impressed with the frequency of the trains, as they seemed to run about every 20-30 minutes.

So, after enjoying the ride through the Alban hills, and seeing the little towns and villages dotting them, just like in some of the paintings you see, we arrived at Roma Termini at about 9:14am. It was a sunny morning, and the temperature was just about perfect, probably around the upper 70's or lower 80's.

We found our way out of the train station, and directly in front of us was Rome. Immediately in front of the station, just across the street, we could see the bus terminal. We wanted to go to the Vatican and the Sistine Chapel first, and my research had told me that the #64 bus was the one to take to the Vatican. It was nick-named "The Pickpocket Express." There's that word again! As we crossed the street, different street hawkers came up to us, offering us various brochures. Since we had been put on alert, we just brushed them off. We did stop at one of the Information Desks and asked where do we catch the #64 to the Vatican, and she told us which platform it was leaving from. So, we walked over to it, and I left Carol there, while I went around the way to a ticket machine to get our tickets. For some reason, this machine would not take my cash or credit card, so I had to go over to one of the manned ticket vendors to buy our tickets. They cost 1.5 euros each. As I was walking back toward Carol, she was hollering out at me. I wasn't close enough to hear her, but when I got to her, she said that she was trying to tell me not to buy the tickets, because she had actually taken a brochure from one of the guys and it talked about the Big Red "Hop-on, Hop-off" sightseeing buses. She had read the brochure and it seemed to her that this would be the best way to get around Rome in the one day we would have in the city. That turned out to be one of the best decisions we made during the entire trip! This bus made a route through Ancient Rome and around central Rome, either passing some of the top attractions like the Colosseum, or having stops near the Vatican and St. Peter's Basilica and the Trevi Fountain among its eight stops. They gave you headphones that talked about all the history that you were passing along the route, and again, you could get on and off at your pleasure, for whatever period of time you purchased. We purchased the 24-hour passes. Additionally, once we got going, we were offered the ability to purchase 'Skip the Line" tickets to get into St. Peter's and the Vatican Museum without having to stand in the long lines. Purchasing these was another great choice, because when we got to the Vatican later and saw those lines, we could easily have spent 3-4 hours just waiting to get into the Vatican Museum.

So, on the bus we went, straight to the Upper Deck. As soon as we reached the top, my wife commented that the view was amazing from up there. We were REALLY tourists now! And as we started driving through the city, I could tell that Rome, it appeared, was going to be the land of Photo Opportunities, unlike any other place I have been to.

Pretty much the first major attraction we came to on the Big Red was The Colosseum, which is in the section of the city called Ancient Rome. The first glimpse of this iconic edifice, that symbolizes Rome and is instantly recognizable, was awesome.

The bus circled all around it, so we were able to get a panoramic, almost 360-degree view. The line looked pretty long, and neither Carol or I had any inclination to get off and check it out from the inside. So, we just kept on trucking on the double-decker.

The next thing on the route that we came to that was kind of interesting was an arch (Arco di Constantino) that the audio told us was the original arch that other famous arches throughout Europe were based on, including the Arc de Triomphe in Paris. Having seen the Arc in Paris, I can definitely see that it was a clone of this one.

We only got a brief view of the columns of the Roman Forum from the bus, so I guess that's one we will have to catch on our next trip.

Before leaving Ancient Rome, the bus passed alongside Circus Maximus. Contrary to what the name implies, it is not really a circus in the sense that we think of today, but it was used to play games of various sorts, and eventually it became Rome's main venue for chariot races. It could hold up to 200,000 spectators, and at times there were as many as 100 chariot races a day held there, with some of these competitions lasting up to 15 days! As we drove along, parallel to the long oval track (about 660 yards or 6.5 football fields from one end to the other), I could just visualize Charlton Heston racing around the track in his chariot in the Ben-Hur movie. The site is used as a park today.

Carol was pretty excited with all of this stuff, as well. She had taken an Art Appreciation class just a few years ago. She said that what she was seeing here in Ancient Rome just from this bus, was exactly what she had visualized Rome to be – from that class – and more! Such grandeur! She started talking about how the tall walls and all the buildings with their Romanesque architecture, including tall pillars and massive columns with the triangular, detailed formations at the top, just brought her class to life!

The audio guide told us to get off at the Castel Sant' Angelo stop if we wanted to go to the Vatican Museum and St. Peter's Basilica. We wanted to, so we did. After crossing the bridge - the famous Ponte Sant' Angelo, completed in 134 AD - to get from the bus drop-off to the Castel, we got a very nice view of it. It has quite a history, as does pretty much everything in Rome, it seems. It was originally built between 123 and 139 AD, so it is quite old. It was commissioned to be built by the Roman Emperor of that time – Hadrian – as a mausoleum for him and his family. Later on, some of the popes used it as a castle and a fortress to help protect the Vatican. Pope Nicholas II even had it connected to St. Peter's Basilica in the 1200's. It really amazes me that some of these old buildings and structures which we have seen, including the Hotel we

25

stayed in while in the Rome area, are still standing after centuries and centuries. That's what made me kind of fall in love with the architecture of the old German castles when I was stationed in Germany while in the Air Force in the late 70's; and that's what really is kind of mind-boggling, if you stop to think about it. They built all these massive structures with all these huge stones, without the benefit of modern lifting technology to help them. That must have been a lot of back-breaking work for the slaves and workers that actually built them. That thought was kind of sobering and sad, though.

After taking photos of the Castel from the bridge, and getting some photos of the bridge itself, we hooked a left and started walking toward St. Peter's and the Vatican. Directions were not really needed because you could see the big dome of St. Peter's from blocks away, assuming there were no other tall structures in the way. There were a few street vendors and mimes along the way, and we got a big laugh from one of them. He had made himself up to be, like "The Invisible Man." His fedora and sunglasses were just kind of floating in the air where his face should be. He did a good job with the illusion (As a matter of fact, he was still there when we returned a few hours later, so I HAD to have Carol take a picture of me sitting next to him, and I dropped a few euros in his bucket).

As we made the right turn onto the side street that led directly to the piazza – St. Peter's Square - in front of St. Peter's, all of a sudden, the crowd density increased tremendously. Another thing that increased dramatically was the sprinkling of soldiers periodically stationed along the routes in groups of two or three, with their sub-machine guns at the ready. Most of these were young men in their twenties, but there were a few young women among them as well. We stopped and asked directions from a young woman who had on a yellow traffic-type safety vest that said "Vatican Staff" and found out that we had just missed the Pope by a couple hours, as he came out on Wednesday mornings to address the people. Rats! Just missed the Pope. That would have been a nice bonus. Oh well…

One thing we noticed as we were meandering around in the piazza was that there were a number of bride and groom couples also roaming around out there. We saw at least four brides in their full length white wedding dresses, complete with their trains trailing along behind them. A couple of them were heading toward St. Peter's Basilica, and a couple were heading away from it. We started speculating and concluded that maybe it was a local custom for brides and grooms to maybe come up to the Vatican on their wedding day to get a blessing, or something like that. But actually, when I got back in the States, and was doing research for background info for this book, I found out that people from all over the world, especially some Catholics obviously, came to Italy to the Vatican area to get married. So, some of the couples we saw may have been foreigners. They actually only do a limited number of weddings at St. Peter's during the course of a year, and you have to apply a couple years beforehand to make that happen. But there are other churches around the Vatican, and throughout the city that foreigners can check out online if they want to make "The Eternal City" their wedding destination.

We took a lot of photos on the piazza, as we wound our way toward the store that we had to get to redeem our "Skip the Line" vouchers. The redemption booth was actually inside a souvenir store/sandwich shop. So, after we got the info about when our tour would leave, we got a couple panini sandwiches and drinks, and I went and sat on the steps at the base of one of the statues outside, to finish my lunch and do a little people-watching.

After finishing our little snack, we went in and checked out the souvenir shop. Mother Teresa of India had just been made St. Teresa about a week before we got there, so I wanted to get a statuette of her. I really did not expect there to be much to choose from though, as her sainthood was so recent, and I was right. The only two statuettes that were left in that store were priced at over 200 euros, and that definitely was not in my budget. But I definitely wanted to get some memento of St. Teresa, since I had always admired the work she had done through the years with the poor and the homeless. So we found a nice little plaque with her picture on it that read, "...Non esiste poverta pegiore che non avere amore da dare... - God bless you, Mother Teresa." The translation of that is roughly, "There exists no greater poverty than not having love to give."

Carol and I both thought that was a pretty profound statement that kind of summed up Saint Teresa's work and life. Carol also thought that those words were especially significant today, when many people look down on the poor.

We got an unexpected bonus at the souvenir shop, as we were able to have our pictures taken with The Pope – or at least a life-size three-dimensional replica of His Holiness. So, we knew that we had received the blessing of The Pope to enjoy the Vatican and the rest of our trip. That was a good thing!

We had to get one last thing at the souvenir shop. That was a scarf/wrap thingie for Carol to wrap around her waist to cover her knees. You could not enter the Vatican or St. Peter's with your knees or shoulders exposed, and Carol had chosen to wear a short blue dress that day that only came down to a couple inches above her knees. So, we paid the 10 euros for that and we were all set.

So now it was 1pm, and time to meet up, so our guide could take us into the Vatican Museum. I guess there were about 30 folks in our party, so after we all got our little sticky thingies to identify us as part of the group, off we went.

Our guide was a rather tall young man, maybe about 6' 2", and it showed as his long legs kept quite a brisk pace. So, despite the thickening crowd, we had to walk pretty fast to keep up. Soon enough, my wife and I wound up sagging until we were last in our group, trailed only by the rear guide, who was making sure no one got left out. I commented to Carol, that I felt sort of like a steer in a herd, with those two guys being the cowboys that were keeping the herd together!

Anyway, we were walking parallel to one of the walls that was an outer wall of the museum we were going to enter. It gave the appearance of being part of a fort, especially with the fact that there were more soldiers with rifles that seemed to be guarding it. It was very long, and we must have walked at least two, maybe three city blocks before we made a left turn. It was a narrow street, and the crowd of traffic going in both directions almost filled it, so that we were almost shoulder-to-shoulder. The crowd had kind of a Mardi Gras feel to it, in regard to density.

As I said, we finally made a left turn, and that's when I realized that some of the people that we had passed before the turn, were part of the line leading into the building. The line was about 3-people wide. And the front of it still could not be seen, because we had, as it turned out, at least another block or two's worth of traveling to go.

We finally came to the end of the wall and saw the entrance, and our guide ushered us into a little open space slightly to the left of the entry door, while he went inside to see about our tickets. It had taken us about 20-25 minutes to get there from the souvenir shop, but we were almost in. However, if we had to go through that line to get in, we'd still be looking at another three or four hours easy!

Our guide came back shortly and led us in through the front door. We were immediately in this large hall with a security checkpoint directly in front of us, some ticket counters off to the left, and a very wide staircase about 20 yards in front and slightly to the left of us. We were herded together one more time, so that we could be given our tickets. As he passed them out, the guide was giving out some kind of instructions, but it was so loud in there, you could not make out what he was saying. I picked out "security" and "food" and "stairs" and "Sistine Chapel" and that was about it. But I wasn't sweating it, because I knew that once we got in, we'd figure it out.

So he said "Arrivederci" and pointed us toward security, and we were on our own. The security there was nowhere as stringent as what you go through at the airports with TSA, so within a few seconds we were in.

It was packed in there – shoulder-to-shoulder people. I saw a sign that pointed upstairs to get to the Sistine Chapel, so that's where we headed. I did not even know what else they had in there, and I really did not care. For my money, as long as we saw the Sistine Chapel, we were good! Carol did not have anything else on her list either to see in there, so up the stairs we went.

At the top of the stairs, they had booths where you could rent audio headsets, so you could do a self-guided, self-paced tour, so we got a couple of those, and were given maps/ a layout of the Museum with that purchase. The Sistine Chapel sign pointed left, so we headed in that direction.

We immediately came into the 1st hall, and the paintings were amazing. The colors, the details, and the clarity were awesome. I had been in The Louvre in Paris a few decades ago, and was instantly reminded of that. We

31

had to go through quite a few more rooms/halls before we got to the Main Event, and some of them had paintings on the ceiling as well.

I did not know what to expect in regard to the Sistine Chapel, other than I knew that the main deal about it was that Michelangelo had laid on his back a few years painting it. So, I can honestly say that when we finally got to the long gallery/hall that contained it, there was no doubt that it was worthy of all the hype and praise it had been given over the years. This was jaw-dropper number one on the trip, for me! The long, narrow chamber, with the barreled ceiling that sort of looked like it converged as you looked further down the hall, was truly amazing. Words cannot describe it.

Carol also thought that the artwork was amazing. The use of gold, yellow and red hues were captivating and made you want to spend hours going through the paintings unraveling what appeared to be small stories-within-stories in several paintings. She further stated that "My appreciation of Rome, having completed an art appreciation class that depicted Michelangelo's work, along with Romanesque architecture, was way beyond expectations."

We spent maybe about only 30 minutes walking down the Sistine Chapel corridor, from one end to the other. One could easily spend weeks, if not months, in there if left alone to study the paintings on the ceiling frescoes alone. But, as my wife said, the flow of the crowd pushing you along was kind of like being on a conveyor belt, so there was no real opportunity to do that. So, all you could do was try to take in a little bit of it, while listening to your headset, as the human tidal wave kept pushing you forward.

We are going to include a couple pictures of the Sistine Chapel here. There's no way the pictures can come close to capturing the true magnificence of this gallery, but they are a start.

After passing through the Sistine Chapel, that was pretty much it. There were some more pretty cool things, like two or three rooms that featured humongous tapestries with the same type of art done on them, as on the canvases. That was quite different. And as we kept following the tour path that was laid out, eventually you are guided through the Raphael Rooms. There's a couple galleries with one of his huge paintings adorning each wall. For a true art lover, this is a big deal, as Raphael is one of the masters, right up there with Michelangelo and da Vinci.

I asked one of the guards who was sitting down in a chair if he had any idea how big this place was. I got lucky because he understood and spoke pretty good English (although I would imagine that most of them probably have to have a grasp on that – but you never know). He told me that you would have to walk about 7.5 kilometers (roughly 4.5 miles) to go through the whole place. I did a little research for this book when we returned home, regarding how this art museum stacks up to others around the world, in comparison to size. When measured by actual gallery space, it comes in at Number Five, with the Louvre in Paris being Number One. But of the Top Ten in that list, it is the oldest museum, having been established in 1506. The Louvre was established in 1792, and the biggest art museum in the United States, The Metropolitan Museum of Art in New York City, which is Number Four in gallery space, was established in 1870. Like I said, everything in Rome is old!

We were pretty much dragging by now. I know we did not cover the full 7.5K of the museum, but we covered a big enough chunk to be shuffling our feet. So, as we entered the last hall in our route before the exit, we were almost halfway through it, before we realized that we were actually inside of St. Peter's. That's why as soon as we entered this hall, one of the officials was shushing everyone, and making sure everyone took a certain route. I really did not care at that point. All I wanted was to see the exit, and start looking for a place to eat. I had walked up quite an appetite!

When we exited the building, there was quite a view in front of us. We were actually at the front entrance of St. Peter's, and we had the view looking out that the Pope and anyone else speaking from those steps would have, looking out over St. Peter's Square. As a matter of fact, they still had folding chairs set up out there. I imagine they were for the Pope's address that morning. This is also the same area from which they conducted the ceremonies when Mother Teresa was made a Saint, eight days before we arrived.

As we exited St. Peter's Square and started walking back up the street toward where we would have to catch our bus, I was hoping we did not have to walk too far before we found a place to eat. We got lucky. After only walking a couple blocks or so up from the square, we spotted an outdoor café area. Almost every table was full, so that was encouraging. We walked over there, and the waiter seated us immediately in one of the two empty tables. Carol headed to the restroom and I ordered a beer, and by the time she made it back, it had already been delivered and I was almost through with it. I guess all that walking must have made me thirsty. It was also probably around 80 degrees outside, so that nice, cold beer was very refreshing!

Carol made it back and we checked out the menu, and ordered our first Italian pizza, with prosciutto and fungi (ham and mushrooms). It was muy delicioso! Oops, is that Spanish, instead of Italian – my bad! One more large beer for me and a glass of wine for Carol and we were good to go.

About halfway through the pizza, another couple around our age plopped down at the table next to us. I could tell they were as worn out as we were.

"The beers are nice and cold," I told the couple. They said that's just what they needed, as they had gotten up early that morning to make it in to see the Pope's address, and after that, and going through the Museum and St. Peter's, they were wiped out. The woman said that she did not even drink beer, but she was going to have one too. They were quite friendly and chatty, and were from Canada. My wife told them that she had never met anyone from Canada, who was NOT friendly, and that brought a smile to their faces. The gentleman pulled out his cell phone to show us the pictures he had taken of the Pope that morning. They had somehow managed to get into about the 2nd row, and the Pope was so close in the pictures, it looked like you could almost touch him. I felt very holy right about then, being that close to someone who had been that close to His Holiness – and I'm not even Catholic!

Shortly after, the woman spotted a friend of theirs that they had come over with, walking toward St. Peter's. She yelled out to her, and she and her husband came over to join them. We exchanged pleasantries and chatted a bit, before they got off into their own conversation. We took a couple last pictures with St. Peter's in the background, and said our goodbyes, and continued back toward the bus route.

We only had one more item on our checklist for this trip to Rome, and that was the Trevi Fountain. So we made our way back to our Hop-on, Hop-off bus, across from the Castel, and after winding around and crossing the Tiber

River a couple times, we came to our Hopping-off point about 15 or 20 minutes later. We were tempted to stop at a gelato store, as we still had not had any yet, but as it turned out, it's a good thing we didn't. We made the 5-minute or so walk down another little side street, and turned a corner and BAM – there it was! A lot of these iconic attractions in Italy were having that effect, we found. They just didn't let you ease into viewing them. They just smacked you in the face with Awesomeness. I know I didn't know what to expect in regard to this fountain. I remember vaguely seeing it in that old movie, "Three Coins in the Fountain" when I was a kid, but I did not expect anything this grand.

This was a relatively new monument, having been completed in only 1762. Some of the sculpted pieces in the fountain looked like Sea Gods, and then there were those horses. And the building itself that backed the fountain! All-in-all, it was just amazing, and I can see why it has such a reputation.

Carol was amazed at the enormity of the fountain and at the number of people who were just sitting there taking in the majestic white travertine statue. It didn't take long before we were drawn into its spell as well.

After we had been there for a few minutes, a young woman asked if we wanted her to take pictures of us with the fountain in the background. Of course, we said yes. So, I sat my package with Saint Teresa down on the ground, and Carol handed her the Canon camera to take some shots. She took a couple, and shortly after, a young guy asked if he could take our picture for us and we handed him one of the cell phones. He snapped a couple, then asked if he could take a couple more with his Polaroid... I said Polaroid. I should have known better, but our guard was down, as we had gone incident-free all day, and had neither seen or heard anything about pickpockets. He wasn't a pic, just a low-level hustler. After he took the Polaroid shots, he asked for a donation to cover his film, blah, blah, blah. Instead of just walking away, I reached in my pocket and pulled out a 5-euro bill and told him to give me three euros back. He started talking some smack about it was 2 for 5 euros, or something like that, and I didn't even argue. He had a handful of change in his hand, so I just reached over and grabbed most of it, and told him to get out of my face. *(In hindsight, I did not even consider how dangerous this could have been. I did not mind giving the guy a couple euros for the photos. After all, that was his hustle. I was just not in the mood to be ripped off!)* Then I picked up my package and we left to catch the Hop-On back to the bus terminal and train station, which was two stops and about five minutes away.

On the way to the Hop-on, Carol, who was walking slightly behind me, spotted a street artist vendor, and before I knew it, she had picked a piece of art she liked from her. The woman said 60 euros at first, and then lowered it to 50, as we started walking away. She came after us, and I told her all I had was 40 USD on me, so if she wanted that, we could deal. She balked, and I told Carol to come on, so we could catch our bus, and needless to say, we got the painting for the 40 USD (about 36 euros)!

As we neared the bus station and put our headsets on, we heard the announcement that this was the last bus back to the station for the day. What! We did not even realize how close we had come to missing our ride, and having to find some other way back, which would have been another little mini-adventure, and quite expensive, I'm sure. As I said, it's a good thing we did not stop for that gelato before going to Trevi!

As we boarded the train after buying our return tickets and validating them, we felt pretty good about our day in Rome. We had DONE Rome, and were ready to kick back and relax the rest of the evening, before getting up the next morning and heading into Tuscany, for the next leg of our adventure. But it seems as though a stress-free evening was not in the cards.

I called our hotel, as the clerk had told me to do, and she told me that at that point, they could not send a shuttle, as the one they used was off on another route somewhere. But she said not to worry, there was a Taxi stand in front of the Train station in Frascati, and we could just catch one there. But when we pulled up to the station and went out to the stand around 30 minutes later, there was no Taxi to be found, and we had no idea when or if any more were coming that evening. So, Carol started talking to the driver of a shuttle from another hotel, and he said he would call one of his taxi-driver buddies to come get us. The guy was there in five minutes, and in another 10 minutes we were pulling up in front of the hotel. And even though I was a couple euros short of the fare (I DID offer him dollars), he just waved it off and said "Grazi, no problem" or something like that. So, all's well that ends well.

We got back inside just before our hotel restaurant was closing at 10pm. We rushed downstairs, because Carol still had a taste for some gelato, so she ordered some to take to the room. No problem. The guy went off to the kitchen and came back in no time… with a bowl of vanilla ice cream! I guess Carol's first Italian gelato would have to wait another day!

9/15 – Hotel Villa Vecchia to Tuscany Lodging – Fattoria Degli Usignoli

W e woke up early Thursday morning feeling great and ready to move on to the next leg of our journey. We had conquered Rome in One Day. Caesar himself could not have done it any better!

Our next destination was Fattoria Degli Usignoli up in the mountains in Tuscany, southeast of Florence. According to what I had mapped out before we left the States, it looked like this projected to be about a 2.5-hour drive from door to door. Checkout was at 10am, and we had packed the night before, so we had all our luggage in the car and were ready to head out shortly after 10. All that was left was to punch the address of our destination in the GPS. But this is where we got the first clue that things might not go as smoothly as we hoped. No matter what combination of the address I punched in, with the Street Name of Localita Piazza and City of San Donato or San Donato in Fronzano, it would not take. I finally just got it to map us with just the City name and since the approximate time and distance were about the same as what I had gotten in the U.S., and since it showed us going in the same general direction toward Florence, we decided to give it a go. I figured that if it got us close enough or into the town, it would still be early afternoon, and I was sure (or at least hoping) we could find someone that spoke English to give us directions. We still had almost a full tank of petro, showing all eight bars, since we had such a relatively short drive from the airport, so I turned the key, and punched the Start button and we were on our way to Tuscany!

It did not take us very long to get on the A1 Autostrada from Villa Vecchia. We had to drive down out of the mountains, and within 15 minutes or so, we were back on flat land, sailing along on this super-highway. We encountered some beautiful landscape scenery as we drove along. There were lots of farms and quite a few grape vineyards as well, which was kind of surprising, because I'm used to seeing grapes up in the mountains, like in Germany. We also passed many olive groves. Although the highway took us through mostly flat land, we could see towns and villages with densely packed buildings, in the mountains off in the distance on both sides of the roads. At one stretch, we passed some buildings that looked as though they were carved out of the mountain.

Around three hours after we started (we had stopped for lunch), we finally saw the exit sign that directed us off the A1.

This is where the Fun starts!

We drove for two or three miles and came to a roundabout, and made our first, of what would be many, wrong turn. This was probably the easiest one to correct because after traveling just a few yards down this path, we could see that it was not a main road (or even a minor road), so as soon as I came to a place where I could pull in and turn around, I did. We quickly got back to the roundabout and took the road to the right out of it, as we should have done in the first place. The sign said we were heading for Reggello and we knew we had to get from Reggello to San Donato in Fronzano, so we figured we were going in the right direction. Our GPS lady had stopped talking now, and the map part of it had gone off the grid, so we were basically on our own at this point.

The road started inclining and getting steeper and steeper and more and more curvy with each kilometer we drove. But after about five more minutes, we were actually in what seemed like the middle of the town or village or whatever it was. Carol pointed to a building with a sign that indicated it might be a post office or something, so I found a place to park, and went inside. There was one teller busy with a customer and one lady in her cubicle on the phone. I patiently waited for the teller and customer to finish their transaction, and as the woman walked away, I started asking the teller if she spoke English. Right about then, another customer walked in behind me, and hearing our conversation, she said that she spoke English. And she did speak it pretty well, I must say. So anyway, I told her we were lost and where we were looking to go, and she quite confidently gave me the directions, saying we were not that far away. As I said, she sounded pretty confident, so I thanked her and briskly walked back to the car to tell Carol the good news. I cranked it up, and made the turns that I thought she had given me, and in about two or three minutes, we were right back where we started!

At this point, I had a light-bulb moment. I decided to call the company that booked our vacation to see if they could get me a more precise address for the hotel. I got through to them on my cell with no problem, but they were not open yet. I had forgot that we were six hours ahead of US East Coast time, so it was only around 8am back there, and they opened at 9. What now? We looked around and saw another building a little further up that looked like it might be some kind of government building. There were no people milling around on the street that we could ask, maybe because there was a slight drizzle. So, I walked over to the building and went inside, stepping into a big foyer. There was a short, stooped-over older gentleman in it, and I walked over to him and asked him if he spoke any English. He did, barely. So, he told me that all I had to do was go up the street that my car was parked on and make a right turn and it would take me right to our lodging. So, I went and told Carol what he said, although after the last set of directions, I was not quite as excited.

So anyway, we drove up a couple blocks and then made that right turn. Everything seemed okay for a while. We drove for about five or ten minutes and the road curved to the right, passing right through what looked like a nice middle-class-to-upscale neighborhood. But again, the road kept getting steeper and steeper with every passing minute.

And then the rains came. It wasn't a super-heavy rain at that time, but it was more than a drizzle. It seemed like the road kept getting narrower and narrower as we climbed. And then the downpour came. It seemed as though someone had cut the bottom out the heavens. It was bad. About this time, the road curved slightly to the left, and when I looked over to my left, I was looking over a cliff and down at the valley across and below. The edge of the road could not have been more than a couple feet from the car, and the road had narrowed down to single-car width. We both had a bad feeling about this. We had not seen any other cars since we left that residential area. We decided that we needed to turn around and get off this road and retrace our steps and start over somehow. But where to turn around? We did not want to keep going for miles and miles. A little bit ahead up to the right, Carol spotted a driveway, which appeared to form a Y as it joined the road on which we were driving. Even though it was pouring, Carol became fearful that there was no end in sight, and that it would get more dangerous if we kept going, so she hopped out of the car and decided to try and give me directions on how to back into this driveway and turn around. It was a very bad angle and very hard to turn around in this V-shape, and it was going to be tough, but again, we did not want to keep going up that road, because we did not know when we would get another opportunity to turn around. So, this was it.

The road was narrow, soft and slippery, as I started easing back and cutting the tail into the driveway. It was on an incline as well, so that did not help. The rain was pouring down at this point, and as I checked the rear-view mirror, I could see it pelting Carol's straw hat as she stood, drenched, behind the car, attempting to give me directions. At about that time, a dog started barking from what must have been the back yard of this property. I had my window down, and that barking must have pushed Carol over the edge. She started bawling like a little baby. I looked out at her, and across at the gulley, and I almost lost it as well. I must admit, that was about the most scared I have ever been in my adult life. I saw death. I fought back the tears. I actually did not know if we were going to make it, and I was just hoping that when I made that left turn to try to get back on the road going back toward civilization, that she steered clear of me in case me and the car went over the cliff. I edged the car back a bit more to try and correct my angle. Now I wish they had given me a little Fiat at Hertz, instead of this big Volvo SUV. Even though Carol was hollering directions to me, I pretty much just blocked her out and was just relying on my own driving skills and instincts at this point. When I finally got my angle right, I gathered myself and gave it a little gas and eased forward, turning left at the same time. My left front tire hit a big stone or something protruding from the left wall of the road, and the car tipped to the right, and slid a little in the mud towards the cliff edge, but I quickly got the left wheel back on the ground and had the entire car sitting in the middle of the road facing in the right direction.

As Carol was standing in the road, hollering instructions that I was ignoring, she said that she saw death. As she continued to get pelted by the rain, she cried out through her tears, "This is the worst vacation I ever had!" Then after I successfully had gotten the car turned, she ran and jumped in the car, still crying. I looked at her, hugged her, took a couple deep breaths, and headed back down the mountain.

After what seemed like about 20 or 30 minutes, we made it back down to the street that we had made the right turn onto to get to our Near-Death Experience. This actually looked like the beginning of another residential neighborhood, so I turned right onto this street and went up to the next street and parked, so we could gather ourselves. Carol was soaked, so she reached in the back seat and got some dry clothes out of one of the pieces of luggage and changed right there in the front seat. I decided to try calling our tour company again, because they should have been open by then, as almost a couple hours had passed since the last time we called them.

The phone started ringing and someone answered. At this same time, a young Italian man in his 20's pulled up and parked in front of the house across the street from us. It had stopped raining now. I gave Carol my cell in case someone answered and I rolled the window down and asked him if he spoke English. And he did. Very well. I explained our situation to him, telling him how we had gotten lost a couple times and where we wanted to go. By now, someone had answered the company's phone back in the States, but just as Carol was about to ask them for an address, we lost the connection. So, the young man said that he could google the name of our hotel to get a phone number and call them for directions. I had tried to get the phone number before we left the States, but could not get it either from the Tour company or online, but he got them and he handed me his phone so I could talk directly to the man who had answered. The man told us what street we needed to turn on, but not knowing which way we were facing, he could not tell us if we needed to turn left or right on it. But at least we had a street name now, so I thanked him, and decided to see if we could find that street. We thanked the young man for his help and gave him his phone back and made a U-turn to head back toward town, because we were pretty sure the street had to be in that direction. In hindsight, I don't know why I did not just ask the young man if he knew where that street was, but we were pretty rattled at that time, and were not clicking on all cylinders. After we had made our U-turn and approached the first street, we passed a house with a van in the driveway with a man in it. Carol asked the man if he knew where that street was, and he said, "That's it right there." It was about five feet in front of us!

So, we made our left turn onto the street, Vallombrosa, and the clerk had told us that all we had to do was just follow it, going through the village of Pietrapiana, and shortly after passing through it, we would see the sign right where the street curved to go into San Donato in Franzano. All we would have to do was take a left at that sign, and we would be on the hotel's property. So, we finally felt like there was a light at the end of the tunnel.

We got to Pietrapiena and there was a fork – two paths to choose from. The one to the left looked like a surface road, or what my wife, being from Jamaica, would call a parochial, or non-main road. So you can guess what happened, right? We took the one to the right. Darn. Wrong again!!!

Long story, short. After traveling about 20 minutes on this road, which again kept going higher and higher and more and more winding, and passing no traffic, we kinda figured we better turn around. We were WAY up in the mountains at this point. There was a slight mist, but we were at an altitude where there were some clouds BELOW us! So, we turned around and went back to that fork in the road, and took the road we should have taken, and Voila, within 15 minutes from getting on the correct road, we were at the front desk, checking in with the woman we had called and gotten directions from earlier. Carol and I kind of looked at each other, because her voice was so deep, all that time, we thought we had been talking to a man on the phone. It was now a little after 6pm, and we had started our journey on this 2.5-hour trip about 10am, eight hours ago!

Feast at Fattoria

W ell, it seems that every Thursday evening, they have a big feast/cookout at our Tuscany home, Fattoria Degli Usignoli. They usually have it outdoors on the property, but since it had rained quite heavily that day, they moved it inside to the ristorante.

Carol and I had just enough time to catch our breath, freshen up, and check out the place a little before heading over to the festival. Fattoria Degli Usignoli was a beautiful property way up in the mountains about 28 km from Florence. It had originally been a farm, lived in and operated by monks back in the 1400's. We had one of the 23 apartments on the property and from both our living room and our bedroom, we had an unbelievable view of the mountains sticking up through the clouds, and of another picturesque village across the mountains. The apartment itself was very rustic, with wooden ceilings with large wooden beams going across them, and large wooden ceiling fans installed. We were on the 2nd floor, so we also had a nice balcony with a table and a couple chairs, accessible from the living room. This was going to be an excellent base for our four days in Tuscany, and a great hopping off point from which to get to Florence and Pisa.

So we strolled over to the ristorante, exploring the grounds as we went. It was a short walk, maybe a couple minutes, but we were able to stop and enjoy the amazing sunset and take a couple of photos of Carol, with the sunset as her backdrop.

As we approached the ristorante, we could hear the music and laughter coming from inside. They were seating people by room number. But to our dismay, when the hostess came to lead us to our seats, she did not lead us to the main room where the activity was, but instead led us to the left to a little side dining room, where some giant wine barrels lined the walls. There were two other couples in there, and they did not look too thrilled about being there either.

After a couple minutes, Carol made some comments out loud about 'How did we wind up in this side room?' and the woman at the next table joined right in. She was fuming. She and her husband were about our age – maybe a little older, and we soon found out they were from Amsterdam. She started talking about how she had certain standards and expectations and did not appreciate being treated like a 2nd-class citizen, being put off to the side. Our feelings exactly! After commiserating with the 2nd couple for a few minutes, about how dark our rooms were in regard to lighting, and about how you had to pay extra if you wanted air-conditioning, and little things like that, Carol asked the third couple how they liked their room. They were a younger couple from New Mexico. They said that they liked their room, and from their description, they had one of the apartments like us. Carol commented to me later that maybe they had not been around as much as us or the other couple, so they may not have had time to experience and develop higher expectations yet.

The next time our waitress passed by, Carol asked her what did we have to do to get to the main dining area? She said that they had two seats available, so she would go prepare them for us. Carol then asked if they had six seats, so all of us could move on, but she said there were only two. So, when she came back to get us, we said our goodbyes to our new short-term friends, and followed her around the corner.

What a difference! The lighting was brighter, the musician was playing up on the stage, and the sounds of laughter and joy were all around us. We would have been miserable if we had to stay in the other area. There was a nice decanter of house wine on the table waiting for us, and I poured a couple glasses. It was a very nice Chianti, with a nice woodsy aroma, and it warmed me up as it went down. We looked around and saw most folks already dining, and so we asked our tablemates if we had to wait to be served or what. They said, no, it was buffet style dining, and the buffets were actually set up on the stage behind the musician, so off we went to the stage!

They had a variety of antipastos, some of which looked familiar, and some which didn't. They also had the famous Tuscan salamis and pasta dishes that the region was known for, along with pizzas. The pizzas were the hot ticket, it seems. I guess people either wanted something they were familiar with (if they were Americans like us) or perhaps they wanted to try something new (if they were from a country where pizza was not so prevalent).

We got back to our table, and after a couple glasses of wine, and some food in our bellies, we started chatting with our tablemates. They were a young couple, probably in their late 20's or early 30's. We soon found out they were from Germany. They were very friendly and we had a nice easy, flowing chat with them. At one point in the conversation, the young lady commented that while they were in Florence, they had seen two people get pick-pocketed within about five minutes. I thought to myself, "Wow, after all this talk about pickpocketing being such a big deal in Rome, I guess we must have been lucky, because I did not see anyone get picked, and no one had tried anything with us either."

Suddenly, the house lights dimmed, and we looked around and saw two of the chefs in their big white chef hats and their burgundy aprons with "Fattoria Degli Usignoli" emblazoned on them, come strolling out pushing two candlelit trays that contained the main attraction of the night – two Roast Suckling Pigs, on a bed of bark and some type of leaf garnish.

When the lights came back on, and they took the pigs back to the kitchen to carve them up, we made our way back to the stage for another pass at the buffet. Talk about eat, drink, and be merry!

When we got back to our table, the young German guy shifted the conversation to American politics. We had intentionally not given this topic or anything to do with news back home, any thought since we landed in Italy. But he told me that he and most of his friends had always looked to America as being the world's leader in terms of democracy and principles. He then asked, "How could you explain Trump supporting someone like Vladimir Putin." I told him that I could not explain it, and that, in fact – to me, it almost bordered on treason. He kind of nodded his head in agreement, and that was the end of our political discussion.

By the time they brought the roast pork out, our neighbors had finished a couple decanters and we were just finishing our first. They ordered one more, and poured a round for the four of us and we all lifted our glasses for a hearty German toast – "Prost!"

The roast pig arrived, served with a side of roasted potatoes and both were delicious. By the time we finished, the hall was almost empty, so we said our goodbyes and headed back to our apartment. It had been a long, stressful death-defying day, and we just collapsed into the bed and were out almost immediately.

Friday, September 16th
– A Chill Day

After all the stress we had been though getting to Tuscany, before we went to sleep last night, I had told Carol that we were just going to stay at Fattoria and chill today. As we rolled out of bed around 10-ish, this seemed like it had definitely been a good decision. The rain was pouring down. At times, the wind was blowing it so hard, that it was raining sideways. I guess that kind of explained that thunderclap that I vaguely recalled hearing overnight. It was probably the loudest one I ever heard, and it seems like it shook the bed too! I remember thinking, "It must have sounded so loud, because we are so close to the clouds, since some of these mountain peaks actually poke through the clouds."

We woke up hungry, so we started snacking on some of the Garrett's Popcorn mix that we had purchased at O'Hare Field in Chicago a few days ago. It was still good, and it held us over until we had Room Service deliver us a couple sandwiches from the bar a little later. They had a limited selection during the daytime hours, as it turned out, but I know that by the time we received them, I probably would have even eaten shoe leather with salt, if that's all they had!

It kept on raining heavily all afternoon, so we alternatively just dozed off, and woke up and looked out the windows at the beautiful mountains until it was time to go down to dinner. We really needed that day to freshen up though, and to recover from our trials and tribulations up in the mountains on our way to this place.

We headed over to the ristorante at around 7pm, as soon as it opened. Carol recalls,

"On our way to dinner, I saw a couple dragging their luggage in the drizzly rain. It was about the same time that we had arrived the previous evening. They looked very frazzled, so I greeted them and asked if they were okay, only to get a story very similar to ours about getting lost in the mountains, on their way here. So we weren't the only ones! They were very upset. I told them that we had gone through the same thing the previous day, and that it WOULD get better."

We then said our goodbyes and continued toward the ristorante. They seated us at our assigned table, but our tablemates were not there yet. I wanted to have something to eat that the Tuscany area was known for, if possible. *Fodor's* had mentioned the area was known for something called *Bistecca Fiorentina* (a thick, T-bone steak, grilled rare). It was supposed to be "the classic meat dish of Tuscany." I saw that on our menu, so that's what I ordered. But I don't like real bloody meat, so I ordered mine medium-well, instead of rare. Carol had *Pici alla Senese* (a traditional pasta dish with cheese and pepper) and a lovely *Insalata di Pomodoro* (Tomato salad). I also ordered a nice bottle of *Nero D'Avola Don Antonio* (red wine), as recommended by the waiter. It's kind of funny. I really don't drink red wines, especially dry ones, back home. But "When in Rome…" – or should I say 'When in Tuscany…"

After a short while, our tablemates arrived. The woman arrived first and she was all bubbly and full of energy. They were a white couple, about our age, or maybe a little older, and they were both dressed very casually (as were we) in sweat tops and jeans. His top said Patriots on it, so it wasn't really a surprise when they told us they were from Boston. He was Terry and she was Pat. They were both attorneys. He kind of reminded me of a local television personality I grew up with in the Chicago-area when I was a kid – Captain Kangaroo. All that was missing was Mr. Green Jeans!

We had a great conversation with them, with each couple sharing stories about what we had done so far in Italy. They told us about this lovely escorted wine-tour they had been on, and it sounded so good, that we told them to leave the info for us tomorrow (Saturday) in case we did not see them, and we might check it out on Sunday, since we already had plans to go into Florence on Saturday. *(When we got back to our apartment Saturday night after a long day in Florence, sure enough, they had stuck an e-mail in our door with all the info necessary to contact the wine tour folks)*

I must say here, for the record, that the T-bone steak they brought out was the biggest, thickest T-bone I had ever seen in all my years. I had seen some thick ones at Hoffbrau House in Dallas a few decades back, but this was a monster! It was succulent, and had a very nice flavor, seasoned just about perfectly.

So, our chill-out day came to an end, and it turned out to be a great decision to just stay on property that day. We were recharged, rejuvenated, and ready for our excursion into Florence the next day!

9/17 – Firenza

As we had learned from the road signs, driving from Rome up to Tuscany, Florence was known in Italy as Firenza. Rome had turned into Roma, and Venice was Venezia. It just sounded like the Italian versions seemed more romantic, with the extra syllables and accents.

We had planned on catching a mid-morning train into Florence that day. We figured that if we started seeing the sights we wanted to see even after lunch, that would give us plenty of time to just hang out and stroll around Florence. After all, there was only one thing we really wanted to see in Florence, and that was Michelangelo's *David*. *Fodor*'s also listed Florence's Duomo as a big deal, so we figured we'd check it out as well.

We had asked for directions to Florence on the same day we checked in, and were given them, along with a nice detailed map of the area we were in around San Donato, and the major roads leading to both Florence and the A1. We were told that Florence was easy to get to. We just had to drive to the train station in San Ellero, which was about a 10-15-minute drive. Then we could park our car there for free and hop on the train for the 30-minute ride to Firenza's main train station, Firenza S.M.N. (Firenza Santa Maria Novella). Sounded simple enough, but so had the other directions we had been given. But, I must give us credit. For the first time on our trip, seemingly, we had no issues getting either to San Ellero, or with catching the train. We did NOT get lost! We left the hotel about 9:45 to catch the 10:14 train, and by about 10:35, we were exiting the train at Firenza S.M.N. It was gonna be a good day!

Firenza S.M.N. was a huge station. I believe that it was even bigger than Roma Termini, the main station in Rome. Or maybe it just seemed that way because we visited it on more than one occasion. It had quite a few stores inside, some of which were the same kind you would see in a typical mall in the United States. There was an escalator toward the middle of the station leading to the lower level. At the base of the elevator was an upright piano, which was available for anyone that wanted to play. During our visits to this station, we heard a young teen-age girl, who was quite accomplished and had a very nice voice, as well. And then later, there was a little kid just banging on it and screaming, as little kids tend to do. And the following day, when we returned to the station to catch our train to Pisa, an elderly Japanese man was playing the piano, doing his best Mario Lanza imitation, but not having much luck!

Since we were not on any schedule, we checked the stores out a bit. We went into a clothing store called Alcott, which Carol had kind of gravitated toward. I was actually a little surprised at how reasonable the prices were. There was a little chill in the air that morning, so Carol wound up buying a light sweat top for herself, and I bought a light hoodie jacket. Carol also picked up a few items of clothing for our granddaughter there. After having a light breakfast of stuffed croissants in one of the cafes in the station, we headed outside to begin our Florence excursion.

When we left the States, there was really only one thing we wanted to see in Florence, and that was David. We had both seen pictures of this iconic figure, and there was really no other reason to go to Florence. The David that the statue was based on was David from the Bible, as in "David and

Goliath" and "King David." But in doing my homework and reading up in Fodor's about what to expect or what to do and see in Florence, it turned out that they had a couple other major attractions. The Cathedral of Santa Maria del Fiore, aka "The Duomo," was one of them. The other was the Uffizi Gallery, which contained many fine paintings, but we figured that between the Vatican Museum in Rome, and the Galleria dell' Accademia here – which held David – we would have had our fill of museums. We decided to check out the Duomo first, since you could see its huge Red brick dome from the train station, and then we would finish our day in Florence at the Galleria since those were our plans, but not actually what happened. So down the station steps and off toward The Duomo we went.

Even though you seemingly could not miss The Duomo because it was so big, because of the density and height of the buildings as we walked along the narrow streets, we soon DID lose sight of it. We kept going in the direction in which we thought it was, but the streets went off at different angles, not necessarily parallel to each other. Before long, after maybe twenty minutes or so, we thought we'd better check with someone since no Duomo was in sight. We had reached a big major intersection which opened up into a huge piazza. We saw a couple young women, maybe in their early twenties, and thought that there was a good chance of them speaking English. And they did. So, we told them we were trying to find The Duomo and one of them told us it was a few blocks and twenty minutes behind us and off to the right. They told us which street to turn on, so back we went. Instead of moaning about how much extra we had to walk, and groaning about how far back we had to go, I looked at this as a "bonus" walk, in which we got a chance to see even more of the city! You never knew what you might run into, so you had to stay positive.

We headed back down the street we had come up on, and made that right turn where she told us to and walked a couple blocks up. We did actually pick up the roof of The Duomo a few blocks ahead. So, we were back on track.

But as we kept walking, we approached a huge building with a large line that obviously HAD to be someplace special. I went over and asked someone in line what that was, and they said it was the Galleria, the place where David was. So since we were right there, we obviously changed our plans on the spot and decided to go in and see David. Although the line was long, it was nowhere even close to being as long as the line to the Vatican had been, so we figured it would probably only take 45 minutes to an hour max. But just as we were settling into our place at the end of the line, a young man came up to us and asked if we wanted to get with his "Skip the Line" tour group. He said they had just two spots left and were getting ready to head inside. Without hesitation, we agreed, and gave him the 30 or 40 euros he was asking for. Talk about good timing! He gave us our headsets and tickets, and took us directly to the front door, where the rest of our tour group was waiting to get in. Having a full group at the ready now, he handed us all off to the woman who would actually be conducting our tour, and inside we went to start our tour.

Almost immediately upon entering, we came to a gallery with some of Michelangelo's sculptures. Our guide was an elderly woman, maybe in her mid-to-late 60's, and she had a calm, reassuring tone to her voice, and was very knowledgeable about the subject matter, which one would expect, of course. She explained to us that these statues were part of Michelangelo's "Unfinished Works." These four statues were almost as famous and significant as David – at least to true art lovers. It was because in them, Michelangelo, by purposely leaving them in various stages of completion, showed the world just how difficult it was to carve human figures out of these giant slabs of marble. It was almost as though they were trying to escape from the marble. When I got back home, I researched these statues, and the names they had been given were "The Awakening Slave," "The Young Slave," "The Bearded Slave," and "The Atlas."

And then, there he was. Turning to the left, and looking down toward the end of a long corridor, there was David in all his glory! To me, this was another of those jaw-dropping moments, and I think this first glimpse of him may have been the highlight of the whole trip for me. This piece was magnificent... and Huge! I later found that it was 17' tall and had been carved from a 6-ton slab of marble from the north Tuscan hills. Michelangelo started working on it on September 13, 1501 and finished in early 1504, about two-and-a-half years later.

Carol said that for her, she really did know what to expect. She said her very first thought was, "They should cover him up with a leaf!"

But after getting over this initial reaction to his frontal nudity, she said that the thing that really struck her was how huge he was – he was "larger than life." She also was amazed at how human and realistic he was, and at the amount of detail. She said it was as though you could see hair-like things on his legs, and the toenails and veins in his arms.

As we got closer to him, you could REALLY see just how big he was. I mean, this is one of those things you see in your lifetime that words really cannot describe. So, I started taking photos with my cell of some of the things that stood out for me. There were the toenails and the veins, as Carol mentioned, but as I walked around David, I realized that I had never seen a picture of his rear-end in any pictures I had seen of him. So, among the pictures I am posting here, you will get a not-too-oft shown view of the behind of David!

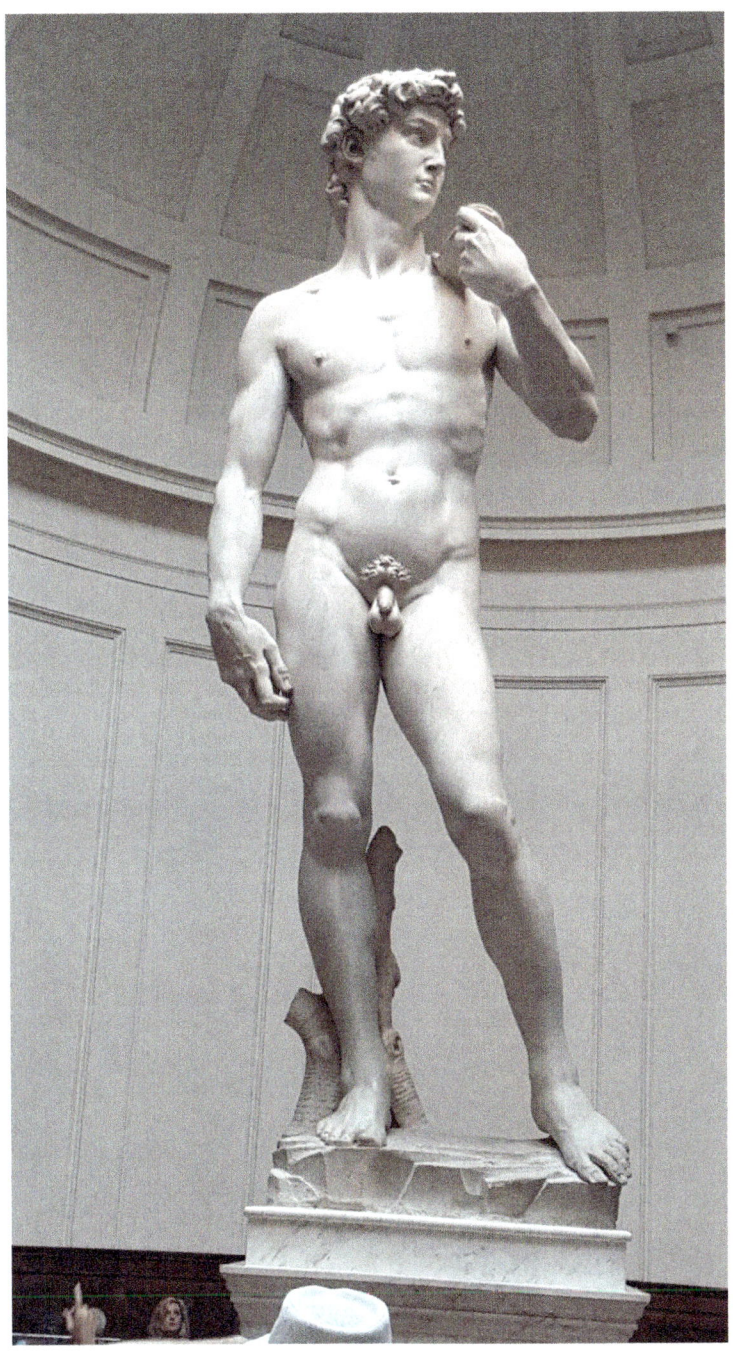

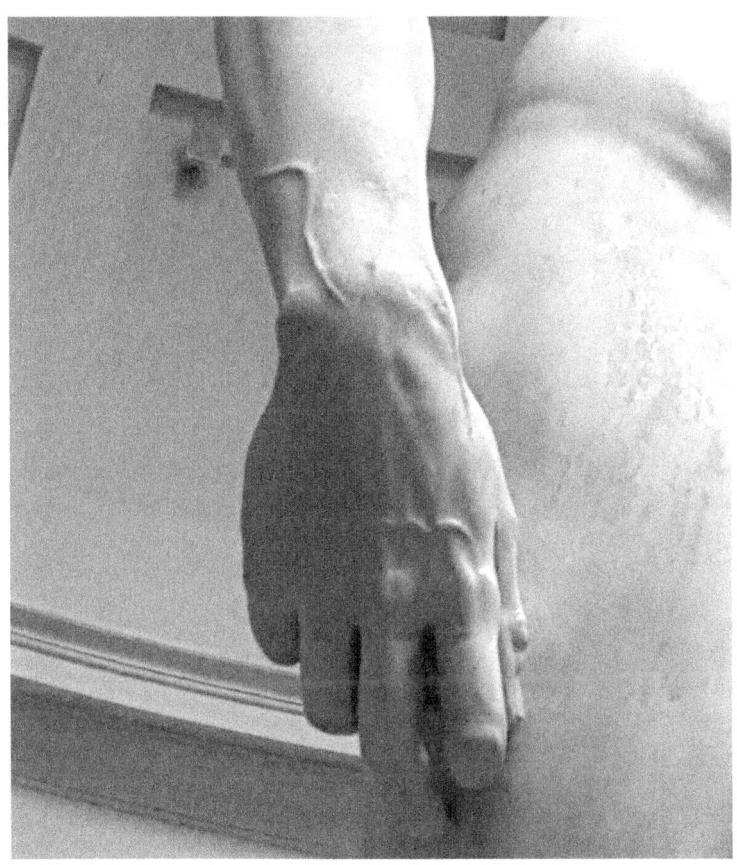

But David was not the only thing of interest in the Galleria. They actually had a Musical Instruments Museum as one of the sub-museums within the gallery walls. Among the things that stood out for me here were a display case showcasing three original Stradivarius violins made by Antonio Stradivari, the world's first upright piano, and a painting of four people enjoying a music session. One young gentleman was at the piano or harpsichord, one was playing a violin, a woman was holding a piece of sheet music, and another young Black woman was listening with a parrot on her arm. I mention this painting because seldom, in all my travels, including to the Louvre in Paris, have I seen a Black person depicted as genteel or cultured in such a manner. I have to reproduce that painting here.

This museum had tons (literally) more of statues and paintings, but for me, those were some of the highlights and items not to miss, or at least to be aware of. We spent almost two hours going through the Galleria, but our stomachs were churning, and we knew it was about time for lunch.

We found a nice outdoor café right around the corner from the Galleria, and on the way to the Duomo. So, we had another lunch of pizza and beer. By this time, my favorite pizza had become "Prosciutto e Funghi" which was Ham and Mushroom. After about an hour or so of leisurely lunch, and people-watching, we headed for The Duomo.

It seems like everything in Italy is either big, or old, or both. The Duomo is a great example. The actual construction on this dome began in 1420 and it was completed in 1436. It weighs 37,000 tons and required 4 million bricks to build it. Along the way, the designer,

Filippo Brunelleschi, had to invent various cranes and hoists that were considered engineering marvels at the time.

There are actually 463 steps you can climb to get to the top of the dome to see the view of Florence from there. Perhaps if we had been 20 or 30 years younger, Carol and I would have tried that climb, but there is no way these old legs and knees of mine - not to mention with the extra baggage I'm carrying around the waist – would have let me make that climb. So, we enjoyed our view from the ground up. And it really was a magnificent one. The dome was attached to a tower that, by itself, was also impressive. And the ornate detail on the building itself added to the grandeur. I'm including a photo below. Sorry for the scaffolding, but they are doing some kind of construction to maybe refinish or reinforce part of the dome. Still, the photo should give some idea of how magnificent it is.

Our final planned stop in Florence was going to be the San Lorenzo market. Our seatmate on the plane to Rome had mentioned this as a place to go for shopping in Florence, and it was also highlighted in Fodor's. It was right around the corner and a couple blocks over from The Duomo. On our way to San Lorenzo, Carol had a taste for some gelato. We had been in Italy for four days now, and still had not tasted any of this creamy delicacy. We had been told that Grom's had the best gelato in Italy, but Carol spotted a young lady who actually was eating a cone with what looked like gelato on it, and asked her where we could get some gelato. She said that she had gotten hers from Eduardo's, which was in the next block and it was even better than Grom's. So, based on this personal recommendation, we headed to Eduardo's. Having not tasted Grom's yet, I could not say which was better, but theirs was really good. I had a mix of three flavors – the Bye-Bye Summer, which included coconuts and banana, Coffee, and Hazelnut and Carol had the same, but replacing the Coffee with Pistachio. Yum, yum, yum!

We walked toward San Lorenzo, happily licking our cones. Clouds were beginning to roll in, so it looked as though we might have to actually use that umbrella we had purchased from a street vendor while we were eating lunch. San Lorenzo turned out to be two or three blocks of shops that had outdoor vendors and tents in front of them on both sides of the narrow street. Some of the vendors were extensions of the stores, and some were just independent vendors who set up their stalls every day. The main items that they had to offer were leather goods – they were promoted in virtually every stall – and knockoff purses – your Pradas and Guccis, etc. We walked down a couple blocks and came to an interesting looking building. What made it really interesting was that we were looking for a restroom right about then, and this public facility looked like it was a good bet to find one. So we did, and Carol paid her euro to go in while I waited. After she came out, we took the escalator upstairs, and it turned out to be like the equivalent of one of our Food Courts back home. They also had a meat market/butcher shop where you could get some of the many varieties and cuts of meat they had to offer, including whole legs or shoulders of beef or pork, which they had hanging. There was also a bar there, so I tried one of the local beers and Carol had a glass of wine and we did a bit more people-watching before heading back downstairs and out.

Just as we reached the street level, the rain started pouring down. Seems like it rained at some point pretty much every day we were there. We ducked into a shoe shop to take refuge, but after about 15 minutes, it still had not stopped, so we gathered ourselves, and opened the umbrella and headed back out. You kind of had to duck from the water running off the canopies on top of the stalls every few feet, but we managed to get through it. As it slackened up, we were approaching the end/beginning of the market area. Carol had noticed some knockoff purses she wanted to check out on the way in, and she saw that same vendor on the way out. So after the requisite haggling, she was able to get a very nice Prada knockoff for a decent price. Having gotten her shopping bug fulfilled, we headed back toward the train station, satisfied that we had "done" Florence!

It was probably about 9pm or so when our train pulled into the station at San Ellero. We felt really good knowing that we were only about 15 minutes away from our lodging, and could just go to the room and chill, and have a relaxing remainder of the evening. All our driving dramas were way behind us. Or so we thought…

71

Near-Death Experience - # 2

So, all we had to do was make a right at the sign before we got into Donnini. It could not have been any simpler. We saw the sign saying Donnini at the fork in the road, about three or four minutes out of the station. So we took the right fork. We drove about maybe a kilometer or two and the road did not seem that familiar. Then we came to a roundabout. Carol said that she did not remember us passing a roundabout on the way to the train station. I didn't either, to tell the truth, but I told her she must not have been paying attention, because we were going the right way. I guess that Male Pride that they always talk about in regard to male drivers must have kicked in, right about then. I just KNEW we were not on the wrong road again. It couldn't be! Off to our left, running parallel to us, but rapidly veering away, and about 20 feet or so higher was another road. That could not be our road, could it? "Nawww."

So, we kept going and in about another kilometer or two, we looked down to the right and saw what looked like an Autostrade off in the distance, and immediately to our right, believe it or not, we saw what looked like a giant outlet mall, with the parking lot all lit up, and the neon lights of some of the stores still on. It was about 9:30 now. There was a Prada store, and some others that I do not recall. But what that outlet mall really signified was the fact that we were lost again! I swung to the right into the parking lot, and pulled over. What now? Well, it was obvious that we had to turn around and go back. So, I pulled out and went up to the roundabout in front of us, and made the circle around it to head back to where we had just come from. Couldn't be that hard. After about 10 minutes or so, we got back to the fork in the road. We had not seen any other roads, but for some strange reason, we decided to go back down the road toward the outlet mall again. Both of us looked at the map that the clerk at the front desk of our property had given us, and we were both convinced that we had to go back down that way. So, we did.

I punched in the address on the car's GPS, but the Italian version of Siri had not been very chatty lately. So, with the address securely entered into both systems, we took off again. Shortly thereafter, we approached the outlet mall again, but this time, we went around the roundabout and exited it on the far side. There was no turning back now. After another five minutes or so, I could not believe what I was seeing on the GPS screen. The upcoming road map had so many squiggly lines switching back and forth! It was unreal. Switchback after switchback after switchback. If that map was accurate, it seemed like we would be doing mountain-road curve turns almost every two or three car lengths. Carol was scared to death and she was freaking out. In talking to her later, she said she wanted to scream because all she could see was death when she looked at that map, but since we were already lost, she said she did not want to stress me any more than I already was. Just when we were wondering if the road would ever straighten out, it did. It actually leveled off, and about 30 or 40 yards in front of us to the right, we saw a restaurant with lights inside and people standing outside. Civilization. We were safe!

It was about 10:30pm at that time. I drove up a little past the restaurant and found a parking spot. I pulled into it, and we both got out, taking our map with us. We had to walk through that crowd of about a dozen or so young folks, but they barely took notice of us. Not very encouraging. The restaurant was divided into what looked like a dining area with picnic tables and regular tables in it, and another side that kind of looked like what you might see on the inside of a QT gas station, only on a smaller scale. So, we walked up to a gentleman behind the counter and showed him our map, and started talking about how we were lost, and needed to get to the location that we were pointing to on the map. It became quickly obvious that he did not speak a lick of English, but he motioned to us to follow him, and he led us back to the same crowd of folks we had just passed through. He gave the map to a young man in a black leather jacket who was probably in his mid-20's, and started talking to him. Sure enough, after that, the young man came over and started talking to us in fairly good English. He told us that all we had to do was make a right turn onto that street right across the street from the restaurant. Then when we got to a dead-end, make a left and keep going till we passed a church, at which time we would keep the road to the right, at which point we would just drive until we saw the Fattoria Degli Usignoli sign. He said we were about two or three kilometers (roughly 1 or 2 miles) away. Since we were starving, and the restaurant on our property was closed by then, we decided to just have a nice pizza right there. The waiter was very friendly, and asked us where we were from. We told him Dallas, and he gave us our menus, and I ordered my favorite – ham and mushroom. It was a very festive restaurant. Seems like a group of about 20 or so were sitting at a table celebrating someone's birthday or something. There was a lot of smiling and laughing going on. We needed to see some of that!

Because the young man who had given us the directions had sounded a little unsure of the directions to Carol, and since we did not want to get lost again, she decided to download Google Maps and punch the address in there. She had refrained from doing so before, because of the fear of running up a huge telephone bill. But at this point, the fear of getting even more lost, and perhaps not making it back, outweighed her fear of losing a few dollars.

We were just about the last ones to leave the pizzeria and it was almost 11:30 when we got back into the car. We followed the young man's directions as given, and did fine until we got to the church. The church was on our right and there was an intersection in front of it. The road to the left looked like a side road, and the one to the right looked a little wider, so I steered to the right. Naturally, it was another wrong choice. In about 20 yards or so, we came to a dead-end, with what looked like a barn directly in front of us and both Google Maps and the car's GPS went off-grid.

There was another car parked down there, and a slender young in his twenties got out. "Great," I thought. "He's coming over to help us."

He did come over and he had great intentions, but no English. He was very animated with his arms, and very impassioned in his direction-giving (or whatever it was he was trying to do), but we could not understand anything. About this time, a light drizzle started. Carol got out to try and help to direct me in turning the car around. (Does this sound like deja-vu to you?) There was not much room to maneuver, but as always, I just used my own skills to maneuver it back and forth, which made her all the more upset, and led to more and more screaming. She said that she was afraid that the guy might rob us, or worse. I finally got it turned, and we drove up toward the intersection. A couple cars were approaching from the same road we had come on when we left the pizzeria. From my angle, I could not make the right turn needed to get onto that road, so I scoped things out, and figured I needed to get into that church parking lot across the intersection, where I would have plenty of room to turn. The lead car of the two kept coming, but then he slowed down, as if to pause to allow me to cross in front of him. So, I eased forward. But then it seems like he sped up as if to ram me, so I had to floor it, and the Volvo literally JUMPED across the road, barely making it into the lot as he made a hard left onto that road. It could not have been any closer. The Lord was surely on our side that night. The fact that I am sitting here recalling and typing about that little encounter is proof of that! Wow!

So, after catching our breaths, I was able to turn the car around in the parking lot. I made that slight left onto the road that we should have been on, and in probably two or three minutes, we saw a street sign saying Fattoria Degli Usignoli. We turned left onto it, and we were home. As it turned out, we had pretty much completely circled around to the South from the train station, taking a back route into town through Cancelli (that's where the pizzeria was), instead of taking that road to the left, which would have taken us on an almost parallel road through Donnini, but entering from the North instead. I had told Carol I would get her home by midnight after we had made our first wrong turn that night, and when we turned the key and entered our apartment, it was about 11:55. Mission accomplished – DOH!

Pisa Anyone?

We slept in on Sunday, getting up whenever we got up. After all, Sunday IS a day of rest. But really, we just slept in because we were tired and stressed from our late-night adventure Saturday night, and we knew that the only thing we wanted to see in Pisa was the Leaning Tower, so we figured that if we did not get over there until around mid-day, that would still be cool.

We had to catch two trains to get to Pisa. First, we had to catch our 'regular' train from the San Ellero station to Firenza S.M.N. Then we had to catch one from S.M.N. to Pisa. Both trips were only about 30 minutes. That was the good thing about Italy, it seemed. You could be in all these beautiful, quaint, rustic towns or villages outside of the main cities, and you could still get to them in little to no time. The combined train travel time from Tuscany to Florence and then Pisa, was actually a little less time than my regular morning commute to work in the Dallas area!

So, we caught a mid-morning train out of San Ellero and got to Florence in time to have a nice leisurely breakfast of croissants and coffee before catching the train to Pisa. We were also able to squeeze a little more shopping in at the Florence station.

When we boarded the train to Pisa, it was already very crowded. We looked down the aisle in the car that we entered, and there were no vacant seats. So, we climbed the four or five steps up to the upper level and found an opening in a compartment that had two 2-person seats facing each other. Carol sat down next to an elderly gentleman in the forward-facing seat, and I sat across from her facing the world that had just passed behind us.

After about 10 or 15 minutes into the trip, the old gent started talking to us. He was speaking English, but I could barely understand him, it was so broken. I figured he must have heard us talking back and forth in English, and was glad to have someone to practice his English on, and he seemed to be a nice guy, so we tried very hard to understand and respond to him. It seems as though he was trying to give us a little history about the area we were passing through, but I can't be sure. The one thing that I do remember and did understand was when he pointed over to a little cemetery off in the distance as we passed it. He said that that was where American and British soldiers who fought and died in World War II were buried. That gave me pause, and made me reflect on my history lessons for a moment. It was hard to believe that war could have been fought in an area as beautiful and peaceful as Tuscany. As a matter of fact, when I thought of World War II and fighting in Europe, I thought of Hitler and the war in Germany. But, as it turned out, in the period between June and August of 1944, the Allies had advanced north of Rome into Tuscany and Florence, and had their last major defensive line in Italy about 48 kilometers north of Pisa. So, it must have been during this time and in that area, that the American and English soldiers who the old man had been talking about, had died. He got off at the last stop before we got into Pisa, so we said our goodbyes.

It was 12:20 when we pulled into the Pisa train station.

As we exited the station, we could see people walking with their umbrellas open, as there was a slight drizzle and it was overcast. We looked across the piazza directly across from the station, and saw a narrow street, from which people were funneling into from every direction. That MUST be the way to the tower. No doubt. So off we went toward that street.

After walking about two or three blocks on the street, we came to an opening and a bridge that spanned a river, the River Arno. We spent about ten minutes on this bridge, as Carol made various adjustments to get her camera ready for the Tower. She had brought her Canon semi-professional grade camera along to take pictures of some of the major attractions, and with the overcast day, she wanted to make sure she had all her settings right. When she was finally satisfied, we started walking again, in the direction that the crowd was going in. The narrow street picked up on the other side of the bridge and went on for another block or two. We finally came to an intersection, where everyone was turning left onto another narrow street.

As we turned onto that street, we saw a couple of young men dressed in uniforms that looked kind of like our West Point Army Cadets. We had seen a few more of them on a couple different occasions at the train station in Florence. They had on light blue pants, with white double-breasted jackets buttoned at the neck, with gold buttons, and the same kind of black caps/hats that our cadets wear when they wear their formal attire. Carol asked them if she could take a picture with them, and they said they were not allowed to do so. Then she asked them who they were, and sure enough, they said they were from the academy. Since it was okay to take a picture of them, I snapped a couple shots and we kept on walking.

The road curved a little to the left, and then – BAM – there it was – clearly leaning off to the left with what looked like a big white church and dome adjacent to it on the right. It was an overcast day, but that first sighting will be burned into my memory forever!

Carol said that the first thing that hit her was how tall it was. And then she was amazed that it leaned so much, and was still able to keep its structural foundation intact, especially the base. (I think maybe she missed her calling, and should have been an engineer!)

When we first spotted it, we were still about two blocks away. It was at the end of one of those same narrow streets, lined with apartments on both sides, some of which had wrought-iron balconies. If any of you have ever been to the French Quarter in New Orleans, that's what the buildings looked like – kind of Old World. But, of course, being over here in Italy, we pretty much WERE in the Old World!

We hurriedly walked those last two blocks and when we reached the end, it opened into a piazza which contained the Leaning Tower and that church off to the left, and a long two-story, yellow building with a large grassy area in front of it, off to the right. We just stood there and took it in for a minute, before getting our camera and cell phone cameras engaged with photo-taking. Of course, we took some of the obligatory pictures of each other with our hands extended as though we were holding the Tower up. That was fun. But the weird thing was, that you had to try to position your camera at different angles to pick up the true lean of the tower. If you took a shot in which the bottom of the picture was parallel to the horizontal ground, you would think that you would be able to see the lean. But you couldn't. Maybe, it was just because we are amateur photographers, but we could not pick up the true lean unless we held the camera or cell phones at exactly the right angle. So, we played around with a bunch of angles until we were satisfied that we had enough photos to do a good Show and Tell when we got back home.

Construction on the Tower began in 1173 and it was completed almost 200 years later, in 1372. It is about 183' tall and looks like a giant layered wedding cake. It is made from marble and weighs about 14,500 metric tons. It has either 294 or 296 steps to reach the top, because the 7th floor has two fewer steps on the North-facing staircase.

The tower's tilt began during construction, caused by an inadequate foundation on the ground that was too soft on one side to properly support the structure's weight. Prior to restoration work performed between 1990 and 2001, the tower leaned at an angle of 5.5 degrees, but the tower now leans at about 3.99 degrees. This means that the top of the tower is displaced horizontally 3.9 meters (12 ft. 10 in.) from the center.

Anyway, after spending about an hour or so around The Tower, we had pretty much covered every angle of it. Plus, we were getting hungry. So, we headed up one of the other many angled streets that seemed to be going in the general direction of the train station, and started looking for a café to grab a late afternoon meal.

As we headed up the street, Carol spotted a guy with a bunch of purses on a pole walking ahead of us. We caught up to him and she scoped out a Smokey Gray Prada that she liked (as a gift for my sister, Dee), so they started haggling. He was rolling a blunt (marijuana/weed/joint) while they went back and forth on the price, but Carol finally wound up getting it for about a third of the original price, so she was happy!

There was no shortage of outdoor cafes, but there was also no shortage of smokers. And unlike back in The States, they did not ban you from smoking at a restaurant, especially the outdoor ones, which I guess kind of made sense. But we had to actually go to two or three cafes, until we found some seats with a view that did not have a bunch of smokers around them. So we settled in. We wanted something other than pizza for a change. When I looked on the menu, I actually saw something I recognized, even though it was written in Italian - *Pappardelle al Cinghiale*. I knew that this was some kind of noodles with wild boar sauce because I had wanted to order it back at the Hotel Villa Vecchia outside of Rome, but they said that they needed about an hour lead-time to prepare it. So when the waiter came, I asked him if it took them that long to make it, and he said no, they had some ready. So I was finally going to get my wild boar meat!

We lucked out here as well. Shortly after we ordered, another waiter (not ours) came and sat a tray of those cured meats and **bread** that were the normal appetizers, on our table. I thought that they were just being friendly, so we started digging in. It included paper-thin sliced hams, salamis, dried sausages, some sweet, and some spicy, and a couple more cuts that we could not identify. What a deal, I thought! And the nice cold beer that I had ordered went perfectly with those cold-cuts. But just as we were finishing, our original waiter came out with what we ordered, and he asked us what the deal was. I told him I appreciated the gift, but he said that the other guy had made a mistake, and since I did not order it, I should have questioned him. I told him Sorry, but I thought that they just brought those trays out to everyone, since I had seen a couple other tables with the trays on them. He just said something in Italian, and walked off. He did not look too upset, but I checked our bill when he brought it to make sure he did not charge us for it. He didn't!

As we meandered back toward the train station after lunch, we noticed a fruit stand with some delicious looking fruit. The white (green) grapes were very big and kind of translucent, actually, almost yellow. So we purchased a couple pounds, and a nice mango that Carol said smelled more 'mangoey' than any she had sniffed since leaving Jamaica. As we popped a couple grapes into our mouths, I thought they tasted like the 'fruit of the gods' and Carol said they were the best grapes she had ever tasted. She decided to save the mango until we got back to our apartment so that she could really savor and enjoy it.

We took our time walking up the street, and just took it all in. It was Sunday afternoon, and along with all the tourists, we could tell that a lot of these people were natives out for a Sunday stroll, whether with their loved one, or perhaps walking their dog, or maybe accompanying their young child on a bike. No one, tourist or native, seemed to be in a hurry. We had noticed that slower pace of life ever since we got into Italy to some degree, but here in Pisa, it was more evident, as there were not as many attractions as in Florence or Rome, which drew more tourists to those areas.

We were back at the train station in time to catch the 5:15pm back to Florence. We then caught one a little after 6pm from Florence and were back at the San Ellero station by 7pm. We were determined not to have any drama or miss any turns on our way back to Fattoria Degli Usignoli... and we didn't!

9/19, On the Road to Venice

Monday was our last travel day, going from Tuscany to our hotel outside of Venice. It was estimated to be about a 3.5-hour drive. We checked out of Fattoria right around 10:30 am and hit the road.

The scenery between Tuscany and Venice was even more beautiful than that between Rome and Tuscany. For over half the trip, it seems, we were actually still in the mountains of Tuscany. We would see patchwork villages and towns up in the mountains, and some of the buildings were carved directly out of the mountains. Amazing! What was even more amazing is that they carved so many tunnels out to drive right through the mountains. We must have passed through at least ten or twelve of these.

Most of them, you were only in for a few seconds, or maybe a minute or so. But the longest one we passed through was about six or seven miles – 6 or 7 miles

INSIDE of a mountain, at a speed of around 70 miles an hour. It seemed like we would never get out of that one. It was two lanes of one-way traffic, as were most of them. It had some lights along the side walls, but it was still pretty dark. When we finally exited that bad boy, Carol and I were like, "Wow!"

After a couple hours of driving, we both started getting hungry, so we began to look for the next Super-Exit/Rest Stop. We had passed one an hour or so ago, and fortunately, soon we saw a sign saying that another one was a few kilometers up the Autostrade. That was great because we had to gas up the car as well as fuel our bellies!

Filling up the gas tank proved to be another example of how the little things we take for granted in the U.S., suddenly become major ordeals in a foreign country. The first thing was, they did not have a place for me to slide my credit card in like we do in The States. I walked all around the pump looking for some way to start it. An Italian guy at the pump next to mine saw that I was struggling, so he pointed in the direction of a building in the back of the huge parking lot. But he must have been watching as I walked in the wrong direction, because he yelled out at me and pointed to my left. I walked in that direction, and there was some kind of master machine that was like the credit-card reader for all the pumps. So, I looked back at my car and saw the number of the pump that we were at, and slid my card in. I punched in the pump number, and walked back to my car, and Voila! - we were all set to pump!

This Rest Stop had a huge two-story restaurant building in it, with the actual restaurant upstairs. We walked up the stairs, and when we reached the top, we saw that it was kind of like a cafeteria/buffet style setup. They had three or four main areas depending on if you wanted pasta dishes, or sandwiches, or whatever. We saw a couple people pass by with trays that had some interesting-looking (and good-smelling) pasta dishes on them, so we got into the pasta line. We both chose a pasta dish that had 3 different types of pasta in it, and cherry-cheese cake looking pastries for our deserts.

The rest of the drive into the Venice region, for the next hour-and-a-half or so, was pretty uneventful. The terrain started flattening out more the closer we got to Venice. It was mostly a lot of farmland. Surprisingly, there were quite a few vineyards on the flat land. We had mostly been used to seeing vineyards in more mountainous or hilly terrains, whether earlier in this trip, or from my time in Germany while in the Air Force. So again, that was a bit of a surprise. We also passed quite a few olive orchards, which was not surprising, what with all of the olive oil that comes from Italy.

It was about 3:30pm when we pulled up to our final home, *The Best Western Villa Pace Park Hotel Bolognese.* There was something reassuring about seeing an American name that we knew – Best Western – as part of the hotel name. It had been a stress-free drive and it was still early, so we decided to take some photos around the grounds before we even went inside to check in. The grounds were very lush, with large beautiful trees, and they also had some more of those statues like the ones we had seen in the museums in Rome and Florence. The temperature was just about perfect on this late summer afternoon. It felt like Fall, even though it was two days before officially changing seasons

After a short time strolling around, we finally went inside. This hotel had the feel of an American hotel on the inside as well. I had read in the brochure before we left the States that it had been built in the 1800's, so it was the most modern of the three places in which we stayed during our trip. We got to the front desk, and the young woman who greeted us spoke very good English. She was very friendly, warm, and accommodating. Carol said she felt at home immediately. We asked her about how long it took to get to Venice, and she whipped out a couple copies of the train schedule and told us it would take about 30 minutes to get to Venice from the train station. She also told us that the train station was just down the street a couple miles, and she gave us directions to it as well. She was easily the most helpful front-desk person we had run into on the entire trip. She even asked us if we would like help getting our bags to the room, and called for a porter to come help us. He brought his cart, and I led him out to the car, where he loaded our bags onto it, and brought them back in. He loaded the cart onto the elevator – it was just big enough for him and the cart – and indicated he would meet us on the 2nd floor. So, we went around the corner to take the stairs up to the 2nd floor, met him there, and he wheeled the cart down to our room. Now THIS was the service we had been used to in our travels, and was the first time we were getting it since we left home! I was happy to give him his well-earned tip.

It was still early, so we decided to make a dry run into town to find the train station so we would know exactly where we had to go the next morning. We also figured we could check out the town while we were down there. The name of the town that we were in was Preganziol. We got in the car and headed back down the main road that we had come in on after getting into town. I had spotted a couple ATM machines on the way in, so I headed back for them, as I knew I needed some more euros. It was a straight shot, probably only a couple miles from our hotel, if that. I saw one of the ATM machines on our right, and was able to pull into a parking space a couple doors down from it. I got my euros from the ATM with no problem, so we started walking up the street to see if we could find the train station. There weren't a lot of folks on the street, but there were some. It was a Monday, and it was a little after 5:30, and it looked like most of the retail stores were closed. We approached a store that looked like a Mom-and-Pop grocery store, so we went in to see if we could get some directions to the station. There was only one person in the store, an employee, and when we asked him, he did not really understand or speak any English. So while we were in there, we looked around, and picked up some more grapes, hoping they would be as tasty as the ones in Pisa.

We exited the store, and went back in the direction that we had come from after leaving the ATM, and I saw a sign that said something about 'statione' that pointed toward a side street. So we headed in that direction, and in a couple blocks, the street ended, and we were forced to go to our right. So, we walked over about a block and crossed paths with a young woman pushing a baby in a stroller. We asked her if this was the right way to go to get to the train station, and in almost perfect English, she told us that, 'Yes, it was just about a block ahead of us and to the left.' We thanked her, and sure enough, after walking about half-a-block, we saw what looked like a parking lot, and as soon as we cleared that corner, we saw the Preganziol Station to our left. It was a very small station, compared to the ones in Frascati and San Ellero, from which we had caught trains into the cities before. We walked over to it and the entrance was at the back of the building (which, I guess, was the front if you were getting OFF the trains). Walking behind the building, we saw one of the now-familiar Ticket Machines, so we were good to go. I got an ice-cream bar from the cooler and we sat down to chill and do some people-watching as I ate it. A couple older gents came up and ordered a couple glasses of wine and took them outside to sit at a table to imbibe and chat. Another young man rode up on a bicycle, which he parked in the bicycle rack, alongside the couple dozen or so that were already there. I guess that a lot of people must have rode their bikes to the train station to catch the trains into the city to go to work. The thing about these bikes, as it was with most of the bikes we had seen around Italy, was that it appears they must have been around 40 or 50 years old. I don't recall seeing one bicycle that looked like it might have been made in the 2000's.

I finished my ice-cream and we left the station, heading back toward the car. We went a slightly different route, because we wanted to check out this large church we had noticed from the street that was in, what appeared to be the center of town. Just about then, a light drizzle started. We looked up and saw a beautiful rainbow, and then right above it, another rainbow. The one on top was not as defined or bright, but it was definitely a cool sight and something you don't see every day. We got some pretty good shots, but unfortunately all we had was our cell phone cameras with us, and not the Canon.

We made it back to the car and returned to the hotel. What a lovely day! This had definitely been the least stressful, and most enjoyable of all our travel days going between one lodging place and the next. We finished a perfect day with a lovely meal at *Ristorante Bolognese* inside of our hotel. I had the *Secondo di Pesce* aka Salmon Trout and Carol had a nice pasta dish, *Pasta Convenzianato.* I asked the waiter, in regard to my dish, which was it – salmon or trout. He said that actually it was a kind of trout found in the rivers in the nearby town of Treviso. It was named Salmon Trout because it had pink meaty flesh, the same color that you normally found in salmon. So with that information, and a couple glasses of the local red wine, we heartily ate and enjoyed a delicious meal, putting the exclamation point on a wonderful day.

Tomorrow – Venezia!

9/20 – A Day in Venezia

I think that this was the day that both of us were looking forward to. Although Carol really enjoyed going to the Vatican and seeing The Sistine Chapel and seeing David in The Galleria in Florence, I don't think she had been as excited as me about those two attractions. I know that she really got into all the Romanesque architecture and such in the buildings and churches, which was as a result of an Art Appreciation course she had taken in college. But we were both really looking forward to Venice. I don't know if it was because it had a reputation of being such a romantic city or whether it was just looking forward to riding up and down the canals in one of those gondolas, or what. But I could even tangibly feel an air of excitement coming from Carol as we drove into town to catch our train.

"Having had a painting in our home that depicts Venice with a gondola going down one of the canals, I was really looking forward to Venice," she said. "But it was even more than I imagined. It was absolutely breathtaking, especially with how the buildings were built up on both sides of the bay as we floated down the Grand Canal. The waves and wakes created by all the water-taxis and water-buses, made it seem like a water highway. Then you could look down as we went along, and it looked as though the canals were actually city streets."

She also was amazed at how buildings that large and tall were able to stand on what really was a series of little islands. She said the engineering that would allow the buildings to stand and withstand the constant beating and pounding from all that water through the centuries was amazing. In fact, there are about 117 islands that make up Venice. She said that even though she had been on many cruises and other vacations, there was nothing really that ever made her have a burning desire to return, but she felt that desire with Venice. She said, after we had returned home, that it was the kind of place that you would want to come back to and just take your time roaming around the city and exploring up and down the canals.

We actually pulled into Venezia Santa Lucia, the main train station, at about 1:45pm. We knew that we wanted to be there to see some of Venice at night, so we did not want to get there too early. The last few minutes on the train were pretty cool because as the train crossed a long bridge to go from the mainland to Venice, you could see some of the other smaller islands that comprised Venice off to the right in the Gulf of Venice that was part of the Adriatic Sea. There were also numerous other train tracks running parallel to ours, and Carol took some photos of them to show our niece, Anika, when we got back home. Anika just joined us last year from Jamaica to attend college in the U.S., and Carol knew that she had never seen so many train tracks before, so she wanted to enlighten her.

As we disembarked from the train and entered the station, almost the first thing that I noticed was a Grom Gelato store. It was about the same size as a KFC that you might see at an airport. I made note of that, because I knew I would have to stop in there before we left Venice so that I could compare Grom's to the Eduardo's gelato we had in Florence.

As we exited the station, we got our first view of Venice. Directly in front of us was a mini-piazza, with the

Grand Canal right behind it. There was a manned ticket booth positioned right on the edge of the water, and on the opposite bank, there was a big white cathedral-like building with huge white Romanesque pillars and with a big green Duomo perched atop it. Off to the left, we spotted the first pedestrian bridge that we saw spanning the channel. Actually, all of the bridges in Venice were pedestrian bridges, because there were no cars allowed. There were *motoscafos* (water taxis) and *vaporettos* (water buses) going up and down the canal in both directions.

After taking this initial viewing in, we looked at each other and smiled. We were really in Venice!

We surveyed the landscape a bit more, and saw that there was a big crowd of people on this side of the canal, down the road to the left a little – right past that bridge. So we headed off in that direction. As we walked, we came upon our first gondola, which was parked at a gondola-station on the canal. It was a long, black shiny vessel, with a heart-shaped black velvet love seat in it. Too cool! We kept on walking and eventually came to a small square with a bunch of stores and a couple restaurants around it. It was almost 2:30 by now and we were getting hungry, so we decided to have lunch at one of the restaurants at their outdoor café. We ordered another pizza, and I ordered a beer. The waiter asked me if I wanted small, medium, or large, and I was pretty thirsty, so I said large. But when he came back with the mug, it was huge – just like the ones that the waitresses carried by the armload over at the Oktoberfest in Munich.

We finished our pizza and headed back down to the ticket booth to get our tickets for the water bus. The buses were relatively cheap and must have held about 70 or 80 people. They were actually just ferries. The water taxis, on the other hand, were a little more private, holding only about 10 people, but they were a lot more expensive. So the water buses or vaporettos, were definitely the cheapest way to get around, if you were going to be going up and down the Grand Canal.

The Grand Canal is actually kind of like the Main Street of Venice. Starting at the train station, it winds around and around for about 2.5 miles, and I was surprised to read that it has an average depth of only about 9 feet. The end of the line is at the Piazza San Marco exit. The ride takes about 35 minutes. Along the way, you pass about 200 palazzi, built from the 13th to 18th centuries by some of Venice's richest families. The palazzi were like mansions, or large homes, but from the water buses, a lot of them looked like 3 or 4 story apartment buildings.

The Canal widened a bit to the right, just before pulling into the Piazza San Marco Exit, and you could see where it opened up into the Gulf of Venice. We exited the water bus, and walked into a huge throng of people. This was like walking up and down Bourbon Street in New Orleans during Mardi Gras! Tons of people.

And there were bridges everywhere. When you looked down the 'street' or one of the many water passages between the buildings, you would see bridge after bridge after bridge. We walked along the main street on the Canal for a while, checking out the people and the sights. At one point, we heard the horn of a cruise ship, and turned to see it glide by as it left the harbor and headed out to sea.

There were lots of street vendors and stalls, and lots of cafes as well, on this main street. Carol saw some original paintings sold by the artist at one of the stands, and earmarked its location, so she could stop back by there to check the paintings out on our way out (although I didn't really know where she was going to put the painting when we got back home).

Fodor's had told me that the Top Attraction in Venice, other than the gondola rides, was the Basilica di San Marco, which was at one end of Piazza San Marco. So, we started off in the direction that I thought it should be in, and after about a 10-minute walk, we arrived at the Piazza. It was a very large piazza, about as large as the one in front of

St. Peter's Basilica and the Vatican back in Rome. As I said, the Basilica was at one end, and if we say that was the East end, then the North, West, and South ends formed a barrier around the square, with a mix of fancy restaurants (of the white-tablecloth variety) and what looked like upscale clothing and retail stores. The restaurants all had indoor and outdoor seating, and at about five or six of them, there were live bands playing.

The Basilica itself was quite grand. It was built in the 11th century, when Venice was under the rule of the Byzantine Empire. It was patterned after the Church of the Twelve Apostles in Constantinople, and is famous for its mosaics.

Another thing that the Piazza was known for was its' pigeons. Feeding the pigeons was supposed to be another "big deal." I did not really take notice of all the pigeons that were milling around on the ground until one flew up and perched himself on Carol's arm. He was quite comfortable there, and obviously, these pigeons were used to being around humans.

The only disappointing moment of the entire trip came for me while we were in the Piazza area. As I mentioned, there were a number of stores around the perimeter. It turns out that there was also a little side street that went out from the back perimeter of the Piazza. We wandered down that street and I saw some shoes in the window of one of the stores that were calling my name. I had not really purchased anything for myself during this trip, but I thought it would be great to go back home with a nice pair of Italian loafers purchased in Italy. And the price marked on them was only about 39 euros. I could not believe it. So, we went in and got with the saleswomanI tried on two or three pairs in different sizes, but we could just not get a pair to fit my feet. I was terribly disappointed, but just sucked it up, and moved on ☺! Oh well, maybe next year in Paris, I can find a deal...

Anyway, we left that store and decided that it was time to go back and do the thing we had really come to Venice for, the ride in the gondola! Fodor's had estimated the price at between 80 – 100 euros ($88 - $110 USD), and at one point, we almost decided that that was too expensive. But I told Carol that there was no way we were going to come all the way to Venice and NOT take a gondola ride. This was a once-in-a-lifetime opportunity, in all likelihood. She reluctantly agreed, although, I know that secretly, she really felt that way too. She just had to keep up her reputation as the miser of the family.

There were gondola-stations all over the place, so when we got back to the main street, we just kind of picked the first one we came to. It actually looked a little fancier and bigger than most of the other stations, with a lot more vessels coming and going. So as we approached, I overheard the ticket guy talking to a prospective customer, and I thought I heard him say 80 euros per couple. I could not believe that, and when he finished with that guy, and got to me, he confirmed that it HAD been 80 euros per couple, but it was now 6pm and the price had gone up to 100. My wife started protesting and walking away, saying that according to her watch, there was still 5 minutes before 6. So he went and talked to his boss, and came back, and we got the ride for 80 euros!

We boarded our gondola, with the gondolier standing inside the boat, and helping us in – Carol first, then me. We had to be careful which side of the boat we walked on as we went back to the loveseat – for balance purposes – but shortly we were seated, and happy. We did not get one of the singing gondoliers, because that was just ridiculously expensive. I told Carol I would sing to her once we got going.

As it turned out, a purchase that Carol had made earlier as we were strolling along, turned out to be one of the best purchases of our trip. She had bought a selfie-stick for about 10 euros, and got a crash-course on how to use it, and that proved invaluable as we undertook our gondola journey. It was really very nice, and may have been the overall highlight of the trip. He took us on a 45-minute trip back through the various canal streets that made up Venice. From the main street looking back, you could not tell how deep back the streets went, or see how they turned at various weird angles once you got up in there. It was as if it were a maze and someone dropped you off in the middle. I can see it taking hours to get out, if you didn't get lost. It was kind of interesting seeing all the boats parked in front of the various residences, just like we park cars in front of our homes. Most of the buildings had a few steps and maybe a stoop/landing that led from the boat to the front door of their building. We passed residences, and some buildings that were stores.

We saw lamp stores, and shoe stores and leather goods and clothing stores. And true to my word, I sang to Carol as we rode along, as she recorded it via our phone perched in its new selfie-stick home.

The canal/streets were just like regular streets, in that at some points, there would be two-way gondola traffic; and sometimes you would run into traffic jams, because of course, the regular people in their regular boats were also traversing the same canal/streets as they went about their routines.

After we had been riding for about 30-minutes, I saw the Bridge of Sighs ahead of us. The Bridge of Sighs is one of the most famous bridges in Venice. The legend is that it connected a palace where prisoners were held in a dungeon to the building where they had to be taken to be executed, and when they crossed over through that bridge to get to their execution location, you could hear them sighing, as they knew their demise was close at hand.

After passing under the Bridge of Sighs, we rode through the canals for another 10 minutes or so before arriving back at our starting point. To me, I had not really known what to expect going in, but I was pleased with both the length of the ride, and the fact that our gondolier took us up and down many of the different side canals. We did not have the singing gondolier, because I am not rich, but it was nice.

I asked Carol what her thoughts were about it, and she said that she was a little scared when we first started out, because we started on the Grand Canal, and were still getting the wake and waves from some of the water-taxis and water buses as they passed by us, so the water was a little choppy at first. But she said that once we got into the little side canals, it was very nice, especially at twilight when some of the lights started coming on from the various buildings along the way, reflecting into the water. She said that was very romantic. She also said that she did not even miss a singing gondolier, because I was singing to her along the way ☺!!

After leaving the gondola, that was pretty much all we had on our list for Venice. Carol did manage to find that artist on the way out, and she purchased three paintings from him – one for us, and two for our daughter Suzette, who would be moving into a new home a couple weeks after we returned to Dallas.

The Final Drama

We got back to the train station in time for us to stop by Grom and get a couple gelatos. The verdict from both of us – although these Grom's were very good, the ones at Eduardo's in Florence were definitely better. So now you know!

We actually caught the 8:45 out of Venice, and were looking forward to a nice, relaxing ride back to Preganziol. After we had been riding for about 10 minutes or so, shortly after the train departed from the 1st stop, I noticed that we seemed to be stopped in a dark field and were not moving. After about 3 or 4 minutes, I mentioned this to Carol, and around that same time, the young conductor came down the aisle and made a statement to everyone, and all I could pick out was the word 'mechanical' or something that sounded like that. So, I asked him if he could repeat in English, and in somewhat broken English, he repeated that the train was having mechanical difficulties, and that they were working on it, but had no idea how long it would be before it was fixed. Oh Great! Just what we needed on our last night in Italy – more drama!

Well, after about 15 or 20 more minutes, the train started moving forward again. No explanation or anything from anyone, but in another five minutes, we pulled into the next station – Venice Mestre, which was the last station on the mainland. When the train pulled into the station and stopped, all the passengers just sort of sat there, because, again, no one had given us any instructions or any clue as to what was going on. But then I guess someone official must have said that we needed to get off, because we started seeing folks walk by who had exited from cars behind us, so we all got up and got off, as well. Everyone started gathering around one of those Arrival/Departure screens like they have in airports, so we did too. I had a schedule with me and knew the number of our train route and I knew we were supposed to be going toward Treviso, so I found another train that was going to be passing through our Preganziol station. It was due in in about another 20 minutes on another platform. We were on Platform 5 and it was going to be on Platform 2, so we had to go down some stairs and across a short tunnel and back up to get to that track. A lot of folks in our car were going in the same route obviously, so we saw a lot of familiar faces when we got back upstairs. I looked on the Arrival/Departure screen again to verify and saw that we were still good, so we just relaxed and started to wait.

But the drama was not quite over yet. Suddenly, we heard a loud plopping sound as if something or someone had fell, and sure enough – we looked around the corner on the other side of a column, and an elderly gent, probably in his seventies, was laying on the ground. A crowd had gathered around him, but he quickly got up after a few seconds. Apparently, he had just tripped over something instead of having collapsed, so everyone breathed a little easier, and commenced waiting. The train got in as scheduled, and about 20 minutes or so later, we pulled into our station at Preganziol.

The parking lot was just a couple minutes away, so we walked over to our car and got in. It was after 10pm, so the hotel restaurant was closed. We were still a little hungry, but I told Carol I was sure there would be some kind of restaurant open in Preganziol, as it was a decent-sized town. And if not, I told her, we could drive up the road to Treviso. I did not have a clue as to what Treviso had, but it was supposed to be somewhat of a major town in this area, maybe next in size to Venice, so I figured we could definitely get something there if we needed to. It would just be our final adventure!

But as soon as we turned onto the main road after leaving the station, I spotted an establishment on the left that looked like it was open. Sure enough, as we pulled closer, we could see that it was a Pizzeria, and the front door was open with a man standing in the doorway. So, I swung into an open parking space, and in we went.

This actually turned out to be a fine-dining establishment. It had deep mahogany-colored walls and hardwood floors, and tables covered with white tablecloths. There was a party of about 10 over in another section of the restaurant, laughing and having a good time. So this was great!

We found a table for two and sat down, and a waitress soon brought a menu over. Even though it was in Italian, I recognized my old standby, Pizza with Prosciutto (Ham) and Funghi (Mushrooms), and ordered half-a-pizza, which Carol and I shared. That was our Last Supper in Italy ☹ ☺.

9/21 – Venice to Toronto to Dallas

W ell, it was all over. We had really done – and survived – nine days in Italy on our own! The last thing to do of consequence was just to get to the airport in Venice and turn the car in. Well, actually, I had to gas up to make sure we turned it in with a full tank, so I went and did that at a gas station just down the street while Carol was taking her shower and getting dressed.

When I got back to the room, Carol was all dressed and ready to go (to my surprise), so all we had to do was take the bags down, turn in the key, and check out. So far, so good. Our flight didn't leave until 11:30, and we wanted to be there a couple hours early. We had been told at the Front Desk the prior night that it was only about a 15 or 20-minute drive to the airport, so we figured if we gave ourselves an extra hour or so, we would be good. So, we pulled off the Hotel grounds at about 8:30.

The drive to the airport was the most uneventful journey we had during our entire trip. That was a good thing! We just had to make one left turn to get out of town, then go down a couple miles to a roundabout that put us on the Autostrade, and sure enough, about 20 minutes after we left the hotel, we were pulling into the airport. We had our eyes open for the Car Return sign. Carol spotted it, and I whipped the car over into that lane and went up a ramp to the 3rd level, and we were good to go.

After turning the keys in, we found our way over to the terminal. It was not the most clearly marked route in regard to getting there, but we and another couple finally found the correct directional markings on the ground, and proceeded to walk the quarter-mile or so to the terminal.

The flight from Venice to Toronto, Canada was uneventful. It was 9.5 hours, so I watched the latest Avengers movie plus one other movie before nodding out, and Carol watched a couple movies as well.

The flight from Toronto to DFW Airport was about 3 hours, and it was even less memorable. We have been back in town a little over 3 weeks as I write this, and I honestly cannot remember anything about that leg of the trip.

Quick Wrap-up

Well, that's really about it. We had a heck of a time on this vacation with a lot of Adventures and a few Misadventures. We saw one of the New 7 Wonders of The World (The Colosseum) and some other attractions (David in Florence, the Leaning Tower, The Sistine Chapel, and the Grand Canal and Venice) that we always wanted to see and that are truly magnificent in their own rights. We got to stay in a lodging in the mountains in Tuscany that was built by monks as a farm in 1406, and stayed in a 500+ years-old hotel outside of Rome. We ate Wild Boar and Green Spaghetti (pesto) and had some of the smoothest, tastiest, cool desert (Gelato from Eduardo's) that we have ever tasted.

Although our Misadventures were pretty terrifying as we were going through them, without them, this would definitely be a less interesting book. Plus, it's always good to look back and laugh at things you overcame or conquered in your life. And we certainly had some of those instances on this trip.

So anyway, in closing, I'd just like to thank you for coming along on this trip with us. I hope that some of what you read may fire you up enough to want to get over to Italy and experience some of the tremendous wealth, breadth, and depth of attractions, art, and architecture that the country has to offer. We just scratched the surface, and it definitely is one of those places you have to go back to if possible. I also hope that we gave you a few tips and insights that will help make your trip more enjoyable, or help you so that you do not have any of our 'Oops' experiences. Thanks again for joining us, and until our next adventure together, from Warren and Carol to you, we say,

"Arrivederci and Ciao Baby ☺ !!!"

Appendix
Observations/Things We Noticed About Italy

➢ Slower Pace overall – No one seemed to be in a hurry; walking at a leisurely pace

➢ People walk a lot; less signs of obesity

➢ They also ride bicycles a lot. But most of the bikes look like they are from the 1960's – they are old!

➢ There were lots of people walking dogs; just about every local, it seemed. They even had the dogs in restaurants – sitting at the tables.

➢ They did not get the "Smoking is Bad for your Health" memo. They smoke a lot, especially the young people.

➢ Breakfast – we did not see any eggs offered anywhere for breakfast. Mostly a lot of croissants – very tasty; filled with fruits or nuts.

➢ Regarding the pasta, Carol commented at one point, it was the "most delicious pasta I have ever tasted."

➢ It's going to be hard to eat American pizza like Domino's and Pizza Hut, etc., after having dined on the super-delicious pizzas all over Italy.

➢ The people were friendly and approachable – unlike the feeling you get in France, for instance, where they seem to kind of look down on you and are rude. At least that's my memories of France from the couple times I've visited Paris.

ABOUT THE AUTHORS

WARREN LANDRUM

Warren G. Landrum, Jr. was born in East Chicago, Indiana. He went off to college to Purdue University, from which he graduated with a degree in Information Systems and Computer Programming. He later received a B.S. in Management from the University of Phoenix.

Warren served in the U.S. Air Force, both at home and abroad. It was during that time that he first became exposed to overseas travel, a passion that he would pursue at every opportunity. While stationed in Germany, he was able to travel throughout Europe, experiencing the various cultures and lifestyles in Holland, Switzerland, France, Luxembourg, Belgium, and England.

Warren continued his traveling ways upon entering corporate America. He had assignments in Bermuda, Taiwan, Bangkok, Thailand (12 trips); and back to Europe again, this time experiencing Paris, Milan, Munich, and the London-Reading area. All of those experiences, along with his leisure travel to various parts of Mexico, Canada, The Caribbean, and throughout the US, along with being married to a Jamaican wife, have truly given Warren a global perspective and insight in regards to both observing and living life!!

Warren's other passions are fishing, which he inherited as part of the Landrum gene-pool/DNA, basketball, and performing as a singer. He founded the Sun Valley Revue, a sextet of talented singer/entertainers that performed 'old-school' R&B music for around two years in the Phoenix area in the late 1990's.

Warren is also the author of four books that have been published - "The Heart & Soul of a Black Man," "Let's Go Home to Indiana Harbor: Reflections From Mid-Town America," "Texas Politics – Grand Prairie Style: Campaign 2013." And the latest one, "Stroke of Grace: The Juaquin Hawkins Story," the autobiography of former NBA and Houston Rockets basketball player Juaquin Hawkins, which he co-wrote with Mr. Hawkins.

Warren works as a Systems Engineer for Baylor, Scott & White Healthcare and has been an IT professional for about 33 years.

In the area of Civic involvement, he ran for City Council in Grand Prairie in 2013 and is also currently a Library Board member for the city, a member of the Rotary Club and a past Grand Prairie YMCA Board member. He is also a member of the Mayor's Roundtable, a select group of citizens hand-picked by the Mayor, who meet periodically with the Mayor to advise him on issues and needs of the citizenry, in addition to making suggestions that can serve to benefit the city, if and when implemented.

Warren is a member of Alpha Phi Alpha Fraternity, Inc., the first Black Greek Letter Fraternity.

Warren and his beautiful wife Carol recently celebrated their 28th Wedding Anniversary and are the proud parents of one daughter, Suzette, and a two-year old granddaughter – Mia.

CAROL LANDRUM

Carol Landrum was born in St. Andrew, Jamaica, in the mountains surrounding Kingston, as Carol Charles.

She majored in Public Health and became one of the first female Public Health Inspectors on the island. She subsequently represented the Public Health Department in the Miss Kingston and St. Andrew Corporation pageant (KSAC), and was a runner-up. The following year, she was selected to act as a contestant chaperone for the Miss KSAC pageant.

Carol migrated to the United States with her daughter Suzette in the mid-1980's. She was living in the Dallas-Fort Worth area, when she met her future husband, Warren

Landrum. The couple recently celebrated their 28th year of matrimony.

Sharing a love of travel, Carol and Warren have had the opportunity to cruise and visit several of the Eastern, Western, & Southern Caribbean islands, and Hawaii and have also spent time together in Asia and Europe. Their most recent trip was to Italy, and that is what inspired the writing of this book. This is Carol's first book as a co-Author, and it is Warren's fifth.

Carol also loves to cook and was featured recently in the local magazine, *Mansfield Now*, in an article entitled, *"In the Kitchen With Carol Landrum."* She is also currently working on her first solo book, a cookbook that will include some of the recipes she has developed over the years.

Carol also pursued a career in Nursing after coming to the States. She obtained her Bachelor's degree in Nursing and has been an RN for 19 years.

Carol and Warren currently reside in the Mira Lagos subdivision of Grand Prairie, Texas, after having spent 12 years in Ahwatukee, Arizona – a suburb of Phoenix. They are the proud grandparents of their first and only grandchild, Mia Marie.

Lightning Source UK Ltd.
Milton Keynes UK
UKOW07f0646211217

314755UK00007B/138/P